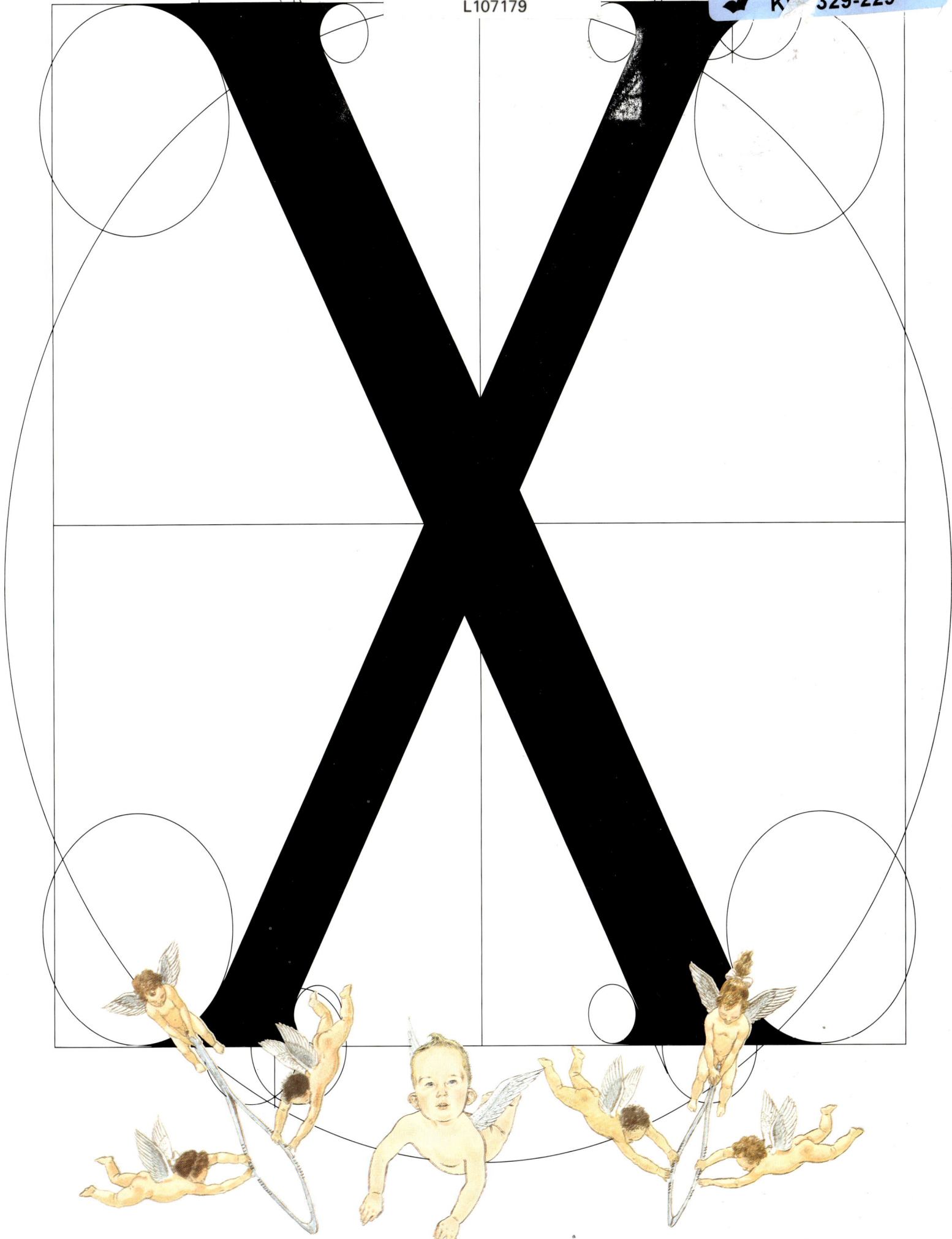

THE X-RAY PICTURE BOOK *of* EVERYDAY THINGS *and* HOW THEY WORK

Author:

Peter Turvey is a curator at the Science Museum, London, where he has worked on a wide range of projects, including the Telecommunications and Space Galleries and the construction of a replica of a Victorian 'calculating engine' designed by Charles Babbage. He studied Physics and Astronomy at the University of Leicester and History of Technology at Imperial College, London. He has also worked as a computer programmer. He is married with two children and lives in Middlesex.

Creator:

David Salariya was born in Dundee, Scotland, where he studied illustration and printmaking, concentrating on book design in his post-graduate year. He later completed a further post-graduate course in art education at Sussex University. He has illustrated a wide range of books on botanical, historical and mythical subjects. He has designed and created the *Timelines*, *New View* and *X-Ray Picture Book* series for Watts. He lives in Brighton with his wife, the illustrator Shirley Willis.

Artist:

Nicholas Hewetson was born in Surrey in 1958. He was educated in Sussex at Brighton Technical School, and studied illustration at Eastbourne College of Art. He has since illustrated a wide variety of children's books. He lives in Brighton with his wife and six children.

First Published in 1994
by Franklin Watts
This edition 2001

Franklin Watts
96 Leonard Street, London EC2A 4XD

Franklin Watts Australia
56 O'Riordan Street
Alexandria, Sydney, NSW 2015

ISBN 0 7496 4142 8

David Salariya   **Series Editor**

Penny Clarke

Book Editor

Artists:
Nicholas Hewetson
Bill Donohoe

Nicholas Hewetson 6-7, 8-9, 12-13, 14-15, 16-17, 18-19, 20-21, 22-23, 24-25, 26-27, 28-29, 30-31, 32-33, 34-35, 36-37, 38-39, 40-41, 42-43, 44-45; **Bill Donohoe** 10-11.

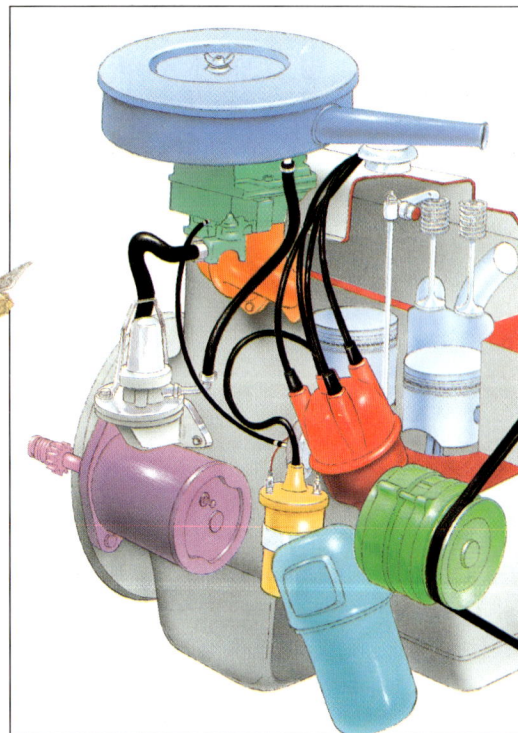

© The Salariya Book Co Ltd MCMXCIV

Printed in Belgium

A CIP catalogue record for this book is available from the British Library.

The X-RAY PICTURE BOOK of EVERYDAY THINGS & HOW THEY WORK

Written by

PETER TURVEY

Illustrated by

NICHOLAS HEWETSON

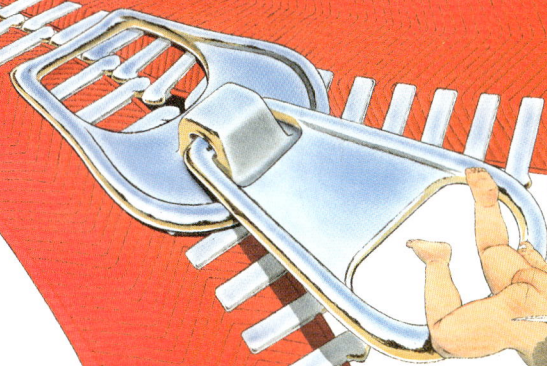

Created
and designed by

DAVID SALARIYA

W
FRANKLIN WATTS
LONDON • SYDNEY

CONTENTS

EASING THE STRAIN

TELLING THE TIME

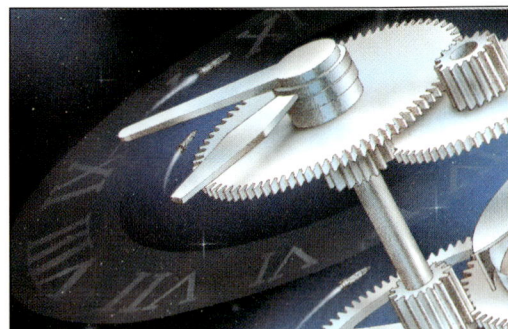

ON THE MOVE

LIGHT AND POWER

TAKING PICTURES

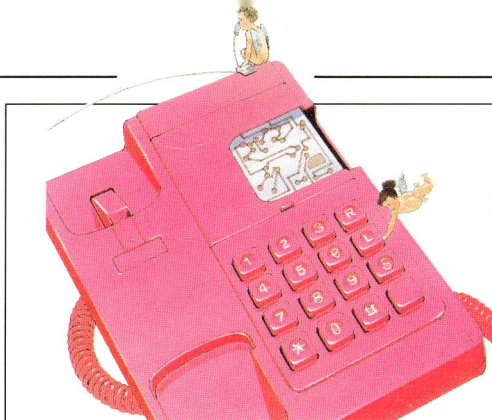

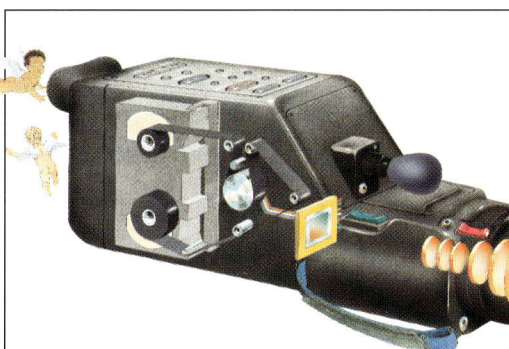

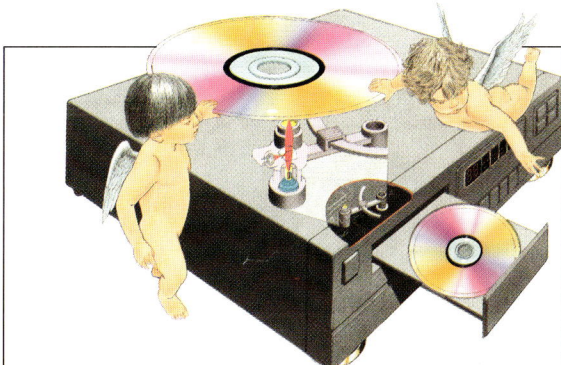

LEVERS

First-class lever

A balance scale is a first-class lever. When the weights (effort) balance the load being weighed, the lever is level.

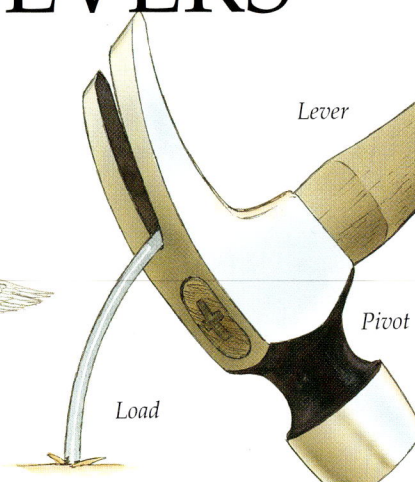

Lever

Load

Lever

Pivot

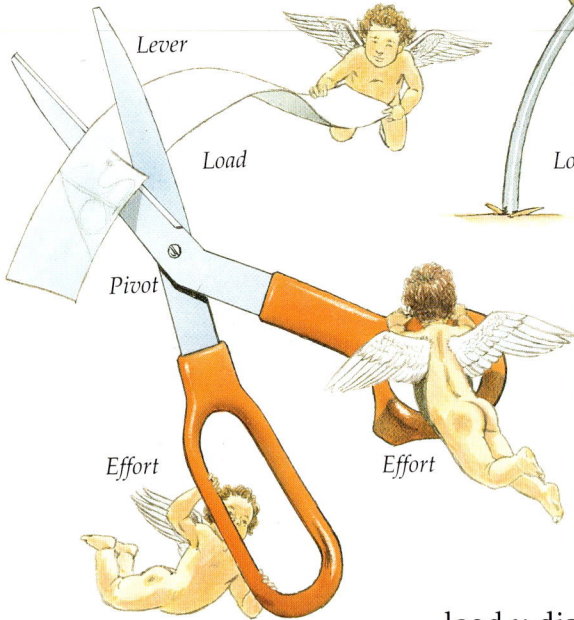

Effort

Effort

Compound first-class lever

Scissors are compound first-class levers. Although each blade of the scissors is a lever, one cannot work without the other. The force exerted on the handles is increased by the lever effect so that the blades cut through things easily.

Lever

Pivot

Load

When a claw hammer is used to pull out a nail, it becomes a first-class lever. The head is the pivot or fulcrum, the nail is the load and the cherub provides the effort.

Levers are among the oldest of mechanical devices. For thousands of years they have enabled us to move heavy or awkward objects relatively easily. A lever is simply a rigid bar which rocks on a pivot or fulcrum. The object to be moved, the load, is placed at one end. Applying pressure, or effort, at the other end of the lever moves the load.

A see-saw is a good example of a simple lever. If you sit on one end of the see-saw it sinks. You are the load. To raise you, someone must apply pressure, or effort, either by sitting on the other end or pulling it down.

The basic principle of levers had been worked out by the Greeks by the 4th century BC. They discovered that the amount of effort needed to move a load was related to its distance from the pivot. In fact:

load x distance from load to pivot =
effort x distance from effort to pivot.

In the case of the see-saw the pivot or fulcrum is halfway along its length, so the effort needed to move the load is the same as the weight of the load. However, move the pivot nearer the load (you), and less effort is needed to move you.

Lever

Load

Pivot

Bottle-openers are second-class levers, with the load (the resistance of the cap) between the pivot and the effort.

Second-class lever

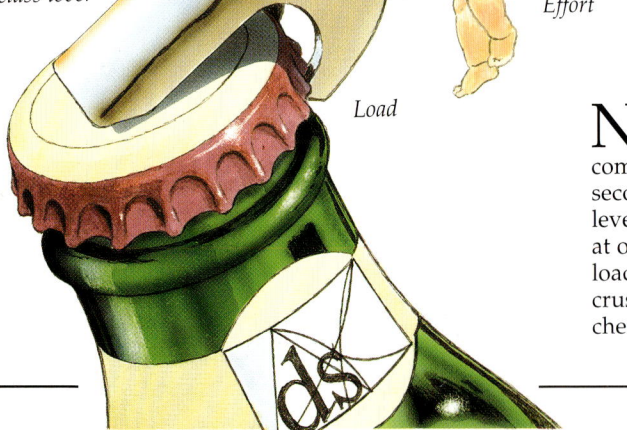

Pivot

Lever

Effort

Load

Nutcrackers are compound second-class levers. Pivoted at one end, the load (the nut) is crushed by the cherubs' efforts.

'Give me somewhere to stand and I will move the earth', said the Greek scientist Archimedes (287-212 BC), who studied the principles of levers. He meant that if he had a long enough lever and somewhere to put the pivot, he could exert enough force to move the earth. Unfortunately, even if Archimedes' pivot was only a metre from the earth, he would have to stand in another galaxy!

There are three types of lever. They differ in the positions of the load, the effort and the pivot. If two levers of the same type are combined using the same pivot, they form a compound lever.

First-class levers have the pivot between the load and the effort. Examples are the see-saw, claw hammer and balance scales. Scissors are compound first class-levers. First- and second-class levers make it easy to move things because they magnify the force we apply. By exerting a small effort you can move a heavy load. The greater the distance between your effort and the pivot (fulcrum) the more the effort is magnified.

Second-class levers are pivoted at one end and have the load between the pivot and the effort. Bottle-openers and wheelbarrows are examples of second-class levers. Nutcrackers are compound second-class levers.

Third-class levers do not magnify force. They magnify distance. They are also pivoted at one end, like second-class levers, but this time the load is at the other end and the effort is between the load and the pivot. So, unlike the other classes of lever, the effort is greater than the load. Your arm when you pick up a weight is a third-class lever and tweezers are third-class compound levers.

Many of the everyday things described in this book use the lever principle somewhere in their mechanism. See if you can find the levers in them. The lever lock is one. The escapement of a clockwork watch contains a lever. The suspension, door locks and steering systems of cars use levers. The mechanism which works the valves of a petrol engine in a car uses them. They are found in electric switches and the mechanism of cameras, tape recorders and video recorders, personal computers and video players. Levers are everywhere – see how many you can find in your home.

Effort

Compound second-class lever

Pivot

Lever

Effort

Compound third-class lever

Load

Tweezers are compound third-class levers, pivoted at one end. The effort to grip the hair (the load) must be applied between the two ends of the lever.

Pivot

Effort

Lever

Load

ZIPS, LOCKS AND INCLINED PLANES

Well over 3000 years ago, the builders of the pyramids in ancient Egypt and the monument of Stonehenge in southern England may have used ramps to lift the stones they used.

Zips get their name from the noise made when they are opened or closed quickly. The first major use of zips was by the US Navy in 10,000 flying suits in 1918.

ZIP-FASTENERS AND YALE LOCKS use the principle of the inclined plane, or ramp, another very early mechanical device. Like the lever, the ramp enables us to do something without using as much effort as we would have to if it were not there. Many shops have both entrance steps and wheelchair ramps. Climbing the steps takes more effort than using the ramp, but you do not have to walk so far.

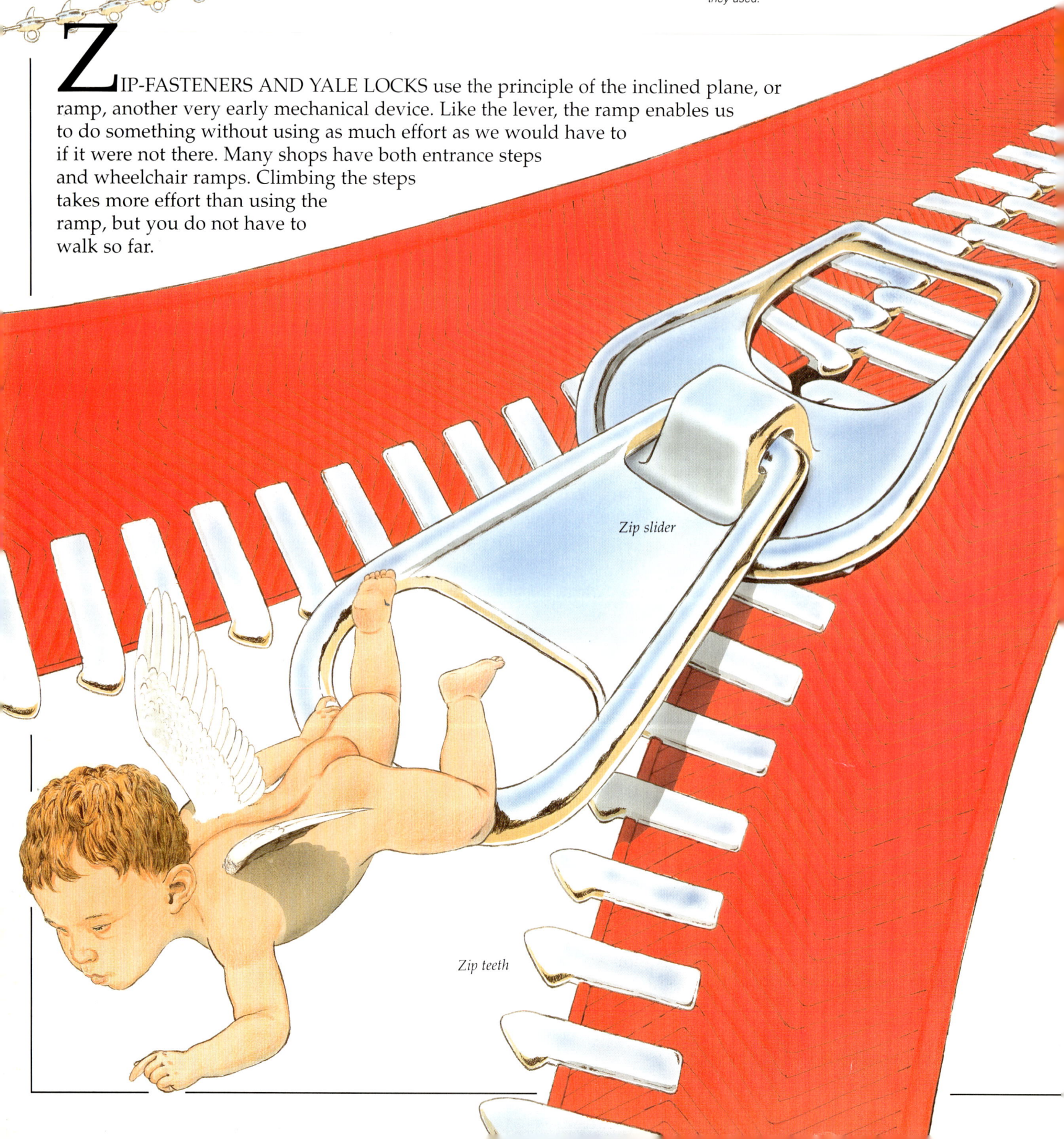

Zip slider

Zip teeth

The first zips had metal teeth and slides. Today, only heavy-duty zips are metal; others have plastic teeth and slides.

Zips have been popular since the 1920s. They are so much easier for small children and elderly people to use than buttons or toggles.

The zip-fastener was invented by the American Whitcomb Judson in 1893. His first design (top left) used an awkward system of hooks and rings closed by a slide. In 1913 Gideon Sundback, a Swedish engineer working for Judson, developed a more practical version, very similar to modern zips. The zip uses the principle of the inclined plane to force together or apart two rows of interlocking teeth fixed onto fabric tapes. The slide contains two outer wedges which force the teeth together when the zip is closed, and a central wedge to push them apart when the slide is pulled back.

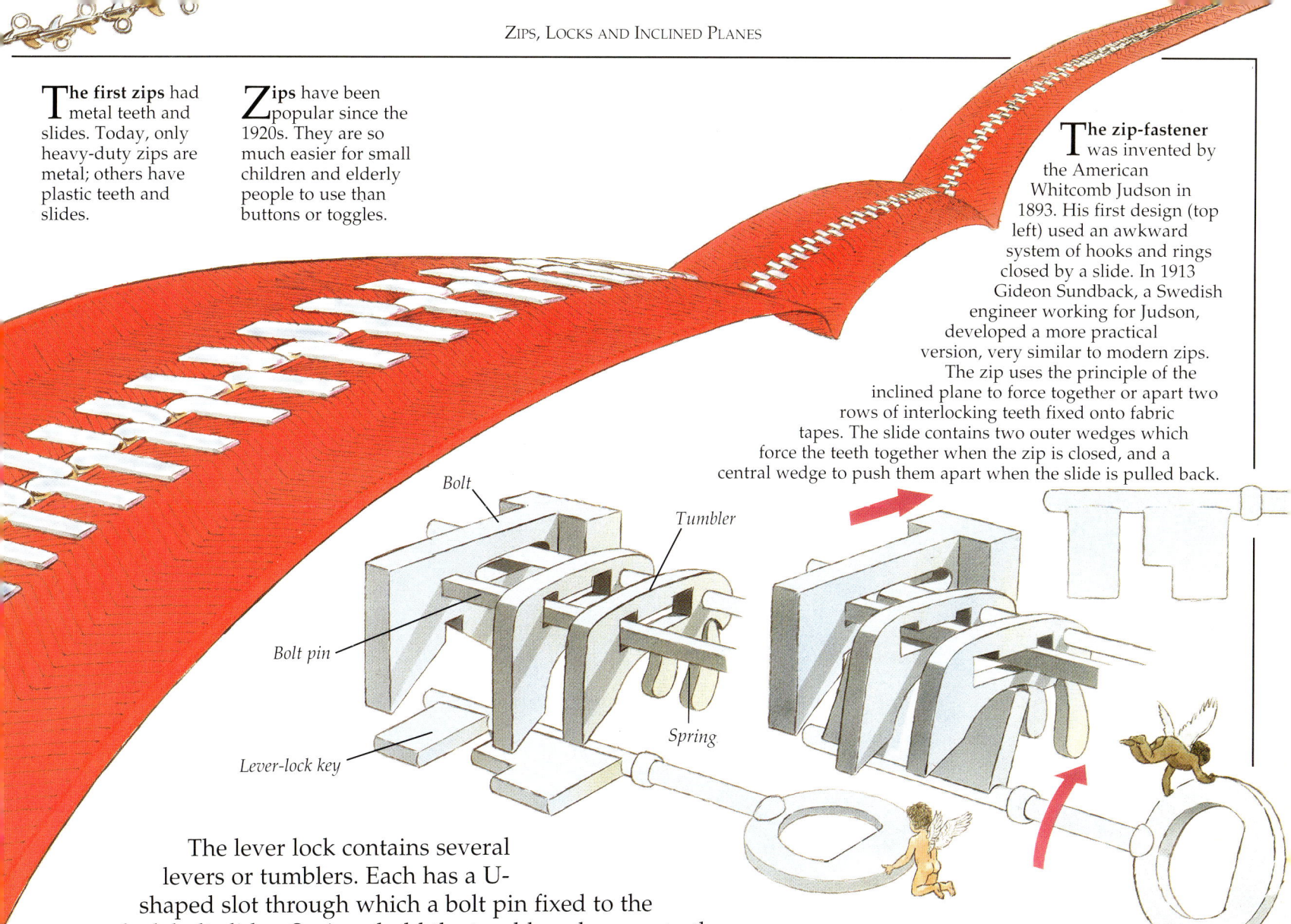

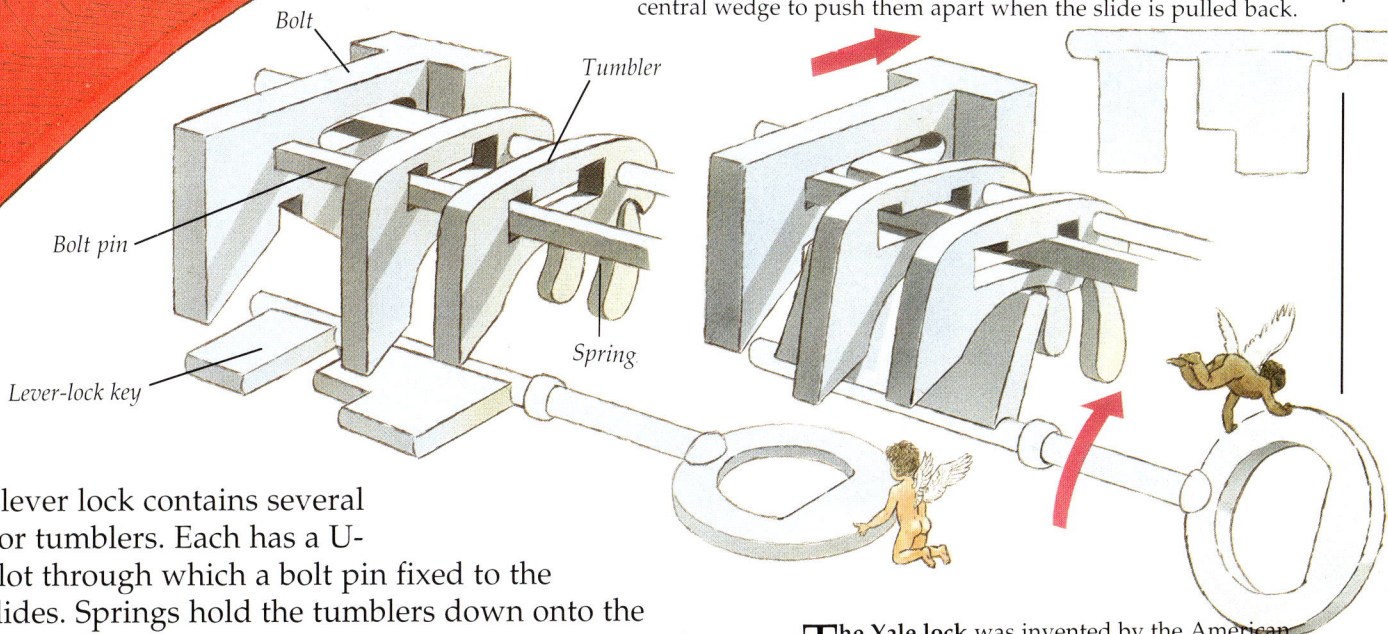

Bolt

Tumbler

Bolt pin

Spring

Lever-lock key

The lever lock contains several levers or tumblers. Each has a U-shaped slot through which a bolt pin fixed to the lock bolt slides. Springs hold the tumblers down onto the bolt pin, to stop it and the bolt moving. The left-hand sides of the tumblers are of different depths. Slots in the key are shaped, so that when the key is turned they lift each tumbler by the right amount to free the bolt pin so it can move along the slot as the end of the turning key catches the bolt and moves it outwards to lock the door. Turning the key further lets the tumblers fall back into place, catching the bolt pin in the other end of the slot, so stopping it and the bolt moving again.

Inside the Yale lock's outer casing is a cylinder. There is a row of holes through both casing and cylinder, each containing a spring and a pair of plungers. The upper plungers are pushed part-way into the cylinder, to stop it turning. To free the cylinder, each pair of plungers must be lifted so that the join between them lines up with the join between casing and cylinder. Each lower plunger is a different length, so each must be raised by a different amount. The serrated Yale key acts as a row of wedges, shaped to raise each plunger by the right amount to let the cylinder turn. As it turns, a shaped wheel, or cam, pushes the bolt into the lock.

The Yale lock was invented by the American Linus Yale Junior in 1848. It is popular as a house and car-door lock. Although the key's ridges are easily copied, patterned grooves along the key's sides make copying more difficult.

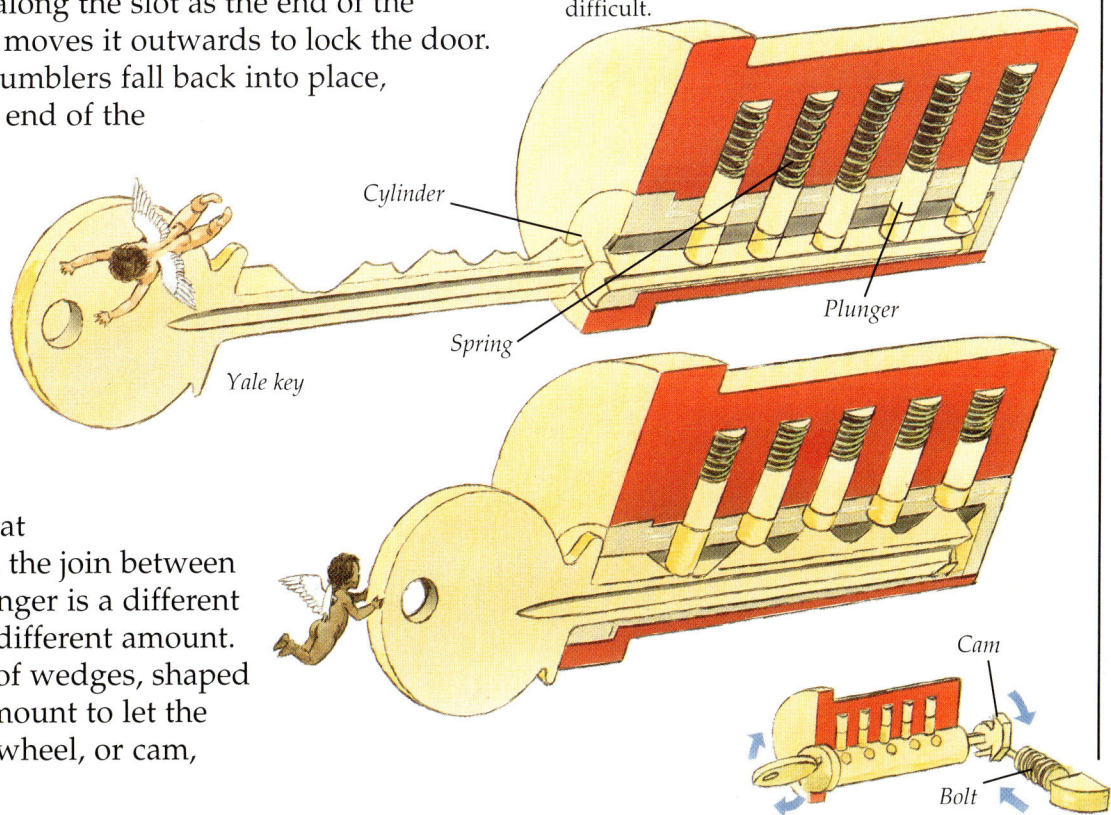

Cylinder

Spring

Plunger

Yale key

Cam

Bolt

Minute hand (fixed to centre pinion)

Hour wheel

Minute pinion

Hour hand (fixed to hour wheel)

Minute wheel

Canon pinion

Centre pinion

Centre wheel

Third pinion

Fourth pinion

Fourth wheel

Third wheel

Escape wheel

Pallet

Barrel

First wheel

Winding button

Winding pinion

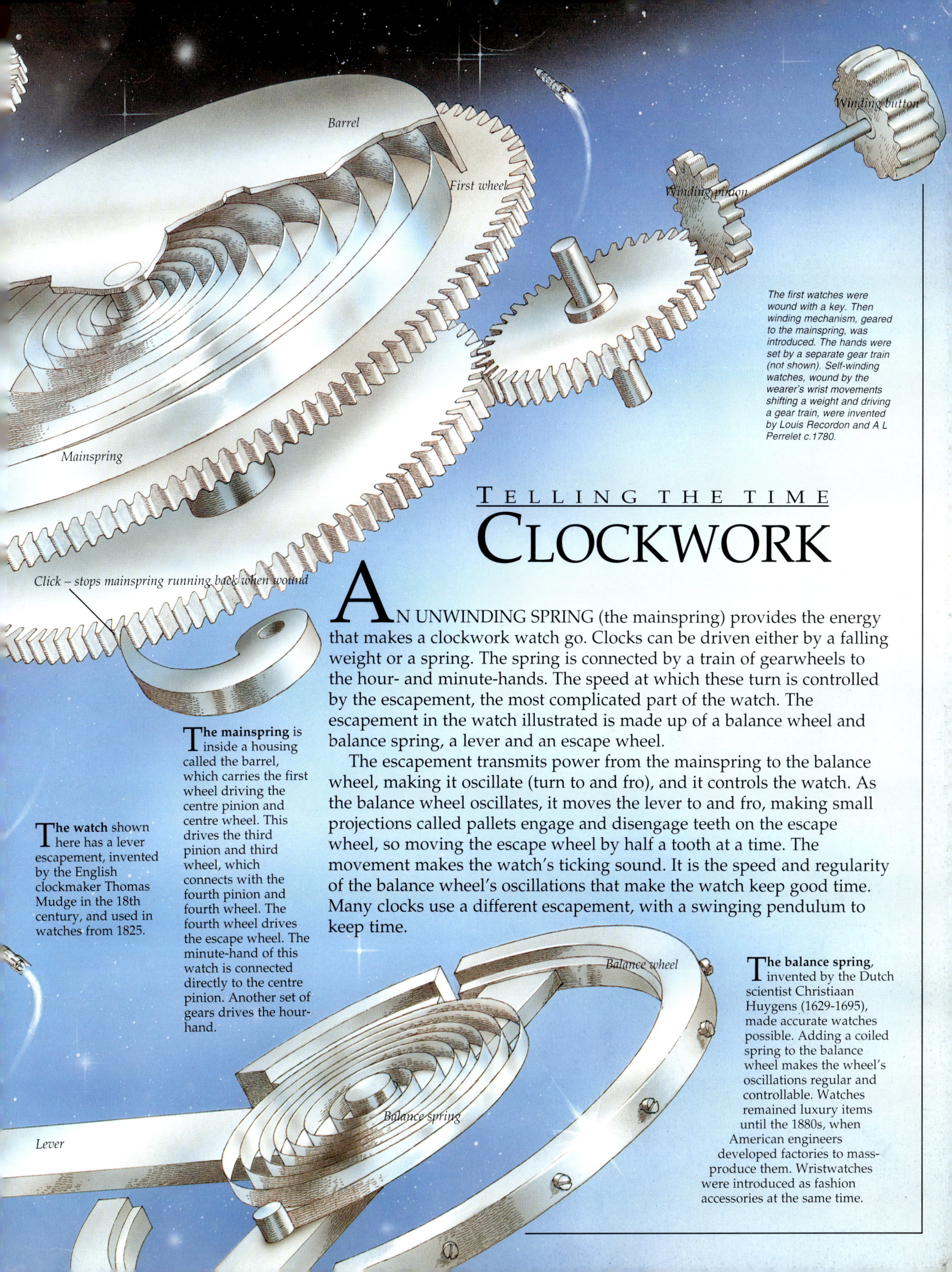

The first watches were wound with a key. Then winding mechanism, geared to the mainspring, was introduced. The hands were set by a separate gear train (not shown). Self-winding watches, wound by the wearer's wrist movements shifting a weight and driving a gear train, were invented by Louis Recordon and A L Perrelet c.1780.

Mainspring

Click – stops mainspring running back when wound

TELLING THE TIME
CLOCKWORK

AN UNWINDING SPRING (the mainspring) provides the energy that makes a clockwork watch go. Clocks can be driven either by a falling weight or a spring. The spring is connected by a train of gearwheels to the hour- and minute-hands. The speed at which these turn is controlled by the escapement, the most complicated part of the watch. The escapement in the watch illustrated is made up of a balance wheel and balance spring, a lever and an escape wheel.

The escapement transmits power from the mainspring to the balance wheel, making it oscillate (turn to and fro), and it controls the watch. As the balance wheel oscillates, it moves the lever to and fro, making small projections called pallets engage and disengage teeth on the escape wheel, so moving the escape wheel by half a tooth at a time. The movement makes the watch's ticking sound. It is the speed and regularity of the balance wheel's oscillations that make the watch keep good time. Many clocks use a different escapement, with a swinging pendulum to keep time.

The mainspring is inside a housing called the barrel, which carries the first wheel driving the centre pinion and centre wheel. This drives the third pinion and third wheel, which connects with the fourth pinion and fourth wheel. The fourth wheel drives the escape wheel. The minute-hand of this watch is connected directly to the centre pinion. Another set of gears drives the hour-hand.

The watch shown here has a lever escapement, invented by the English clockmaker Thomas Mudge in the 18th century, and used in watches from 1825.

Balance wheel

The balance spring, invented by the Dutch scientist Christiaan Huygens (1629-1695), made accurate watches possible. Adding a coiled spring to the balance wheel makes the wheel's oscillations regular and controllable. Watches remained luxury items until the 1880s, when American engineers developed factories to mass-produce them. Wristwatches were introduced as fashion accessories at the same time.

Balance spring

Lever

Watching the changing lengths of shadows cast by sticks was a very early way of keeping track of the time.

An Egyptian clepsydra, or water clock: c.1400 BC. The bowl has a hole in the base; marks on the inside show the time.

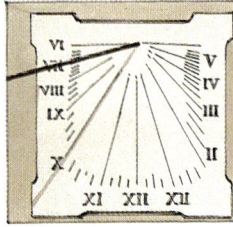

Sundials were developed from the Egyptians' shadow clocks about 1500 BC. The ancient Greeks also used them.

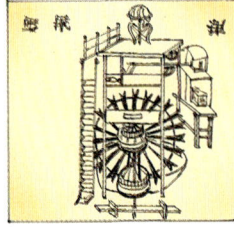

The Chinese had mechanical clocks centuries before the Europeans. This is Su Sung's clock of 1088, driven by water power.

A design for an ornamental clock, carved on the back of a model elephant by the Arab engineer Al-Jazari in the 13th century.

A European weight-driven clock made around 1450, with a bell for striking the hours and a dial with an hour-hand.

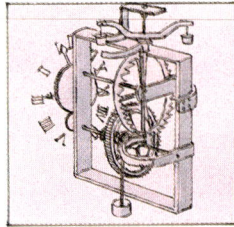

The earliest mechanical clocks did not have hands. Instead, each hour bells rang to mark the passing time.

A portable, spring-driven table clock made by the French clockmaker, Nicholas Lemaindre in 1619.

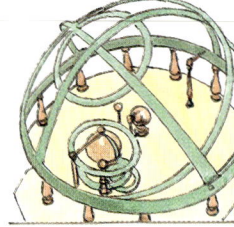

An 18th-century orrery, a clockwork model of the solar system, shows the movement of the planets round the sun.

Clocktowers were distinctive features in towns. This 16th-century one, in Ulm, Germany, is one of the most elaborately decorated.

TELLING THE TIME
KEEPING TIME

THE ANCIENT EGYPTIANS were the first people to divide the day into a fixed number of hours, although their hours varied in length. They also invented the shadow clock (ancestor of the sundial) around 1500 BC and the water clock about 1400 BC. In China, from the 8th century AD, the mechanism of early clocks was moved by water tipping from buckets at regular intervals. In Europe equal hours were adopted only when mechanical clocks came into use in the 14th century. These mechanical clocks were only accurate to about an hour a day. It was not until the Dutch scientist Christiaan Huygens (1629-1695) built the first pendulum clocks in 1656 that really accurate timekeeping became possible. Minute-hands were also introduced at this time. The English scientist Robert Hooke (1635-1703) also developed a balance spring. This made it possible to build accurate portable clocks.

Today, mechanical clocks are almost obsolete. Most clocks and watches use a quartz crystal, made to vibrate accurately and continuously by an electric current. The crystal produces an electrical signal which either drives the hands of the clock or watch or shows the time directly on a Liquid Crystal Display (LCD).

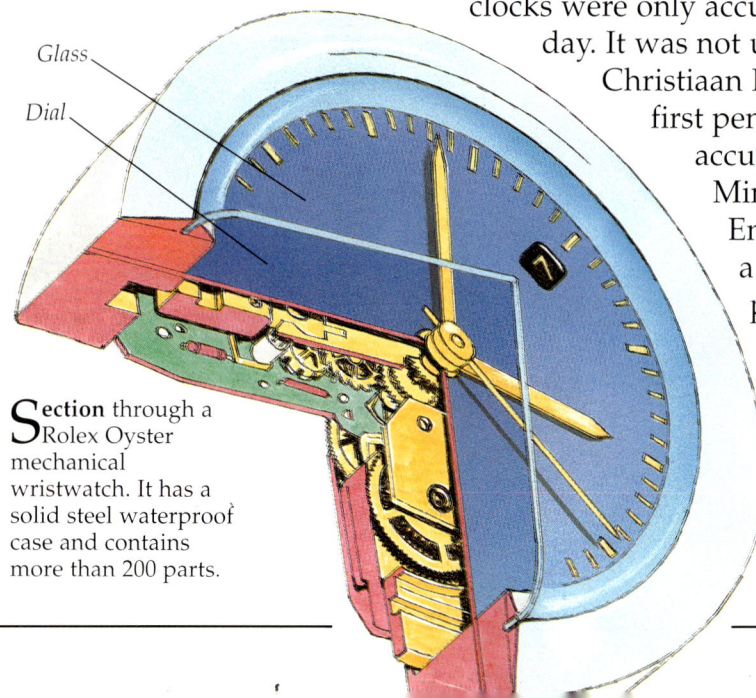

Miniature clocks became possible after the invention of the spring-driven clock around 1450. The first watches, spring-driven clocks small enough to be carried easily, were made in Nuremberg, Germany, about 50 years later. These early watches, nicknamed 'Nuremberg eggs', were worn on a chain around the neck. Pocket watches were popular until the First World War, when artillery officers discovered that smaller wristwatches were easier to use.

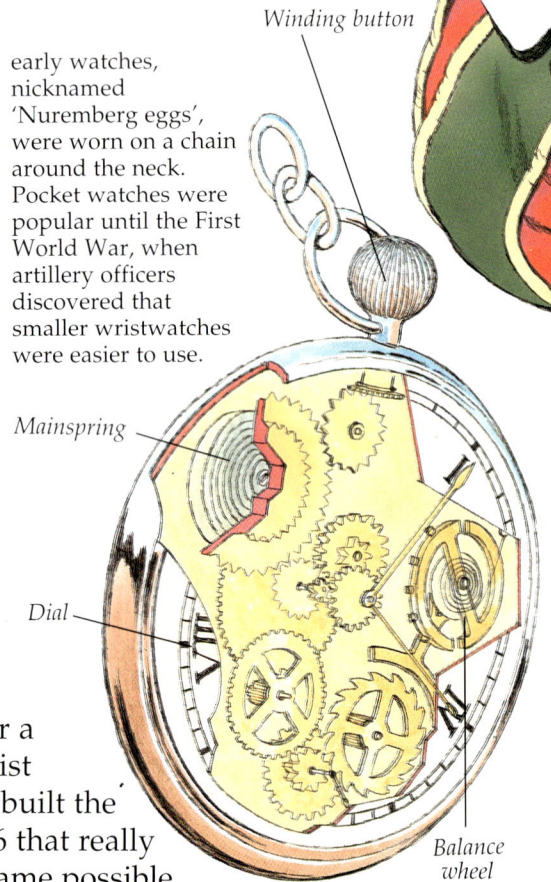

Winding button

Mainspring

Dial

Balance wheel

Glass

Dial

Section through a Rolex Oyster mechanical wristwatch. It has a solid steel waterproof case and contains more than 200 parts.

Inside the trumpet-player's body are two sets of springs connected by chains to conical drums called fusees. These ingenious devices, developed in the 1400s, compensate for the decrease in power as the springs wind down. They are connected by gearwheels to a drum with pins which work levers attached to a series of bellows which blow air through the trumpet. The position of the pins programs the tune played.

Bellows

Drum with pins to work bellows

Fusees

Winding handle

Springs

The invention of the spring-driven clock led to many other inventions using springs to provide power. The wheel-lock gun, developed in the 1500s, was one. In this gun a spring spins a serrated wheel against a piece of iron pyrites to make sparks to ignite gun-powder and fire the gun. More peaceful and amusing uses were automata, mechanical figures driven by clockwork which played musical instruments, played chess, walked or 'ran' about.

ON THE MOVE
THE CAR

MOST OF THE KEY FEATURES of the modern car were invented before 1900, although they have been improved since then. Today's car is essentially a strong, light steel shell surrounding the passenger compartment, the engine and other systems. A suspension system connects the wheels, with their four pneumatic tyres, to the body, and absorbs shocks from bumps in the road. Power is provided by an internal combustion engine, either petrol- or diesel-fuelled. Power from the engine drives the wheels via a transmission system, which incorporates a gearbox, so that the car's speed can be varied, while keeping the engine running at the best speed and allowing the car to be reversed if necessary. The braking system slows the car down. The electrical system operates lights, horn, windscreen wipers, fans and starter motor.

Laminated safety glass, which cracked rather than shattered, was introduced in 1905. Modern cars use toughened glass, which shatters into relatively blunt fragments.

Seat belts stop drivers and passengers being thrown forward in a collision. They are an important safety feature.

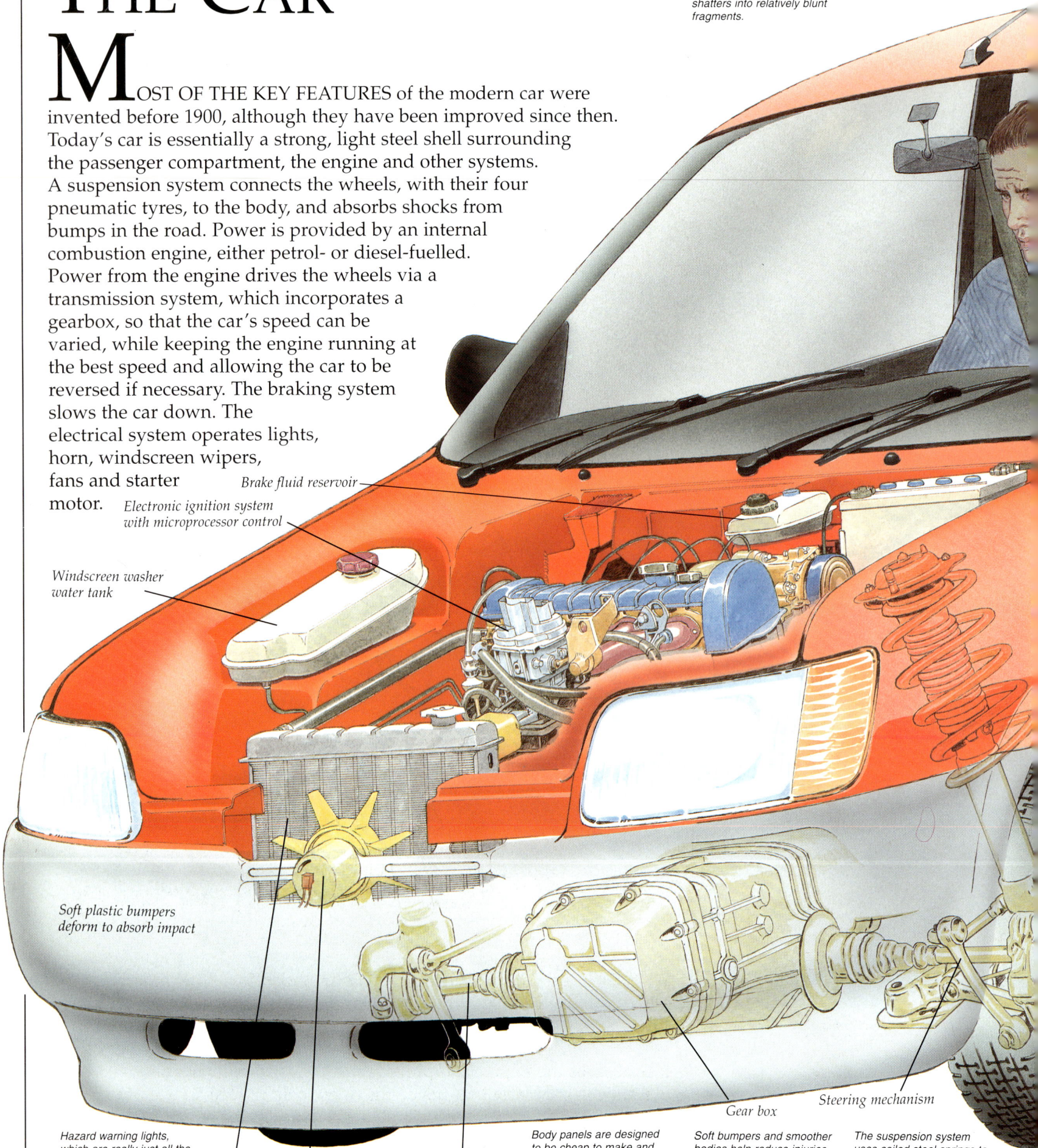

Brake fluid reservoir

Electronic ignition system with microprocessor control

Windscreen washer water tank

Soft plastic bumpers deform to absorb impact

Gear box

Steering mechanism

Hazard warning lights, which are really just all the direction indicators flashing at once, can be switched on in an emergency.

Radiator

Engine cooling fan driven by electric motor

Drive shafts to front wheels

Body panels are designed to be cheap to make and easy to repair. Streamlined designs reduce 'drag', so cars use less fuel.

Soft bumpers and smoother bodies help reduce injuries to pedestrians. Mascots on cars like Mercedes and Rolls Royces fold back.

The suspension system uses coiled steel springs to cushion road shocks. Shock absorbers stop the car rocking as the springs flex.

Streamlined body design makes cars more efficient

Child seats fix in car to carry children safely

Head restraints fitted to seats help stop whiplash injuries caused by the driver's and passenger's heads flying back if the car is struck from behind.

Petrol filler flap locks to prevent theft

Anti-burst door locks – do not fly open in a crash

Car doors contain stiffening bars to protect passengers from side impacts

Rear suspension fixed to car structure

Wheels unbolt to replace easily if tyres are punctured

The 'Mini' made front-wheel-drive cars popular in the 1960s. Today, most cars are similar, with engine and gearbox in one compact unit.

Roller bearing in wheelhub

Front brakes

Brakes worked by a foot pedal act on all four wheels. The handbrake operates only on the rear wheels.

The grooved pattern on a tyre's tread forces water out and maintains grip in wet conditions. Steel wires within the tyre's walls give it strength.

Some cars have anti-lock braking. A microprocessor controlling the brakes senses when a wheel is about to skid and momentarily releases the brake on that wheel.

The car's steel shell has strengthened attachment points for engine, suspension system, seats, seat-belts and bumpers. Assembly is mostly on robot production lines.

Today's saloon cars are designed to make the best use of interior space. Outside, only essential rear-view mirrors disturb the smooth outline.

Safety is an important feature of car design today. The body of a modern car contains a strong steel cage to protect passengers. The roof pillars are strong enough to prevent the roof collapsing if the car rolls over. The front and rear of the car are deliberately designed to collapse in a crash. This absorbs the impact and protects the 'cage', so reducing injury to passengers. Stiffening bars inside the doors help reduce damage caused by side impacts. Anti-burst locks stop the doors flying open in a crash, but are easy to open afterwards. Other safety features, such as seat-belts, head restraints and safety glass, are standard fittings. In the end, however, safety often depends on drivers.

Timing belt — *Camshafts*

Valves

Pistons

Crankshaft

Flywheel

Power from the pistons reaches the crankshaft through the connecting rods. The camshafts, driven by a timing belt from the crankshaft, work inlet and exhaust valves.

ON THE MOVE
THE PETROL ENGINE

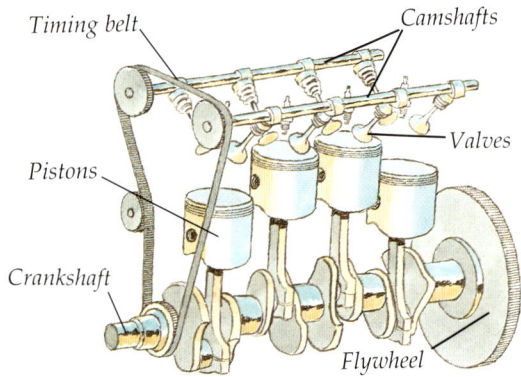

MOST CARS ON THE ROAD TODAY are powered by internal combustion engines fuelled by petrol or diesel. (Buses and lorries mainly use diesel engines.) In petrol engines, which are the most common car engine, the fuel passes first through a carburettor, where it is mixed with air which contains the oxygen needed for combustion (burning). The mixture then passes into the cylinder and is ignited by an electric spark plug. The expansion of the burning gases forces the pistons down and, via connecting rods, turns the crankshaft of the engine which is connected to the car's wheels through the transmission system.

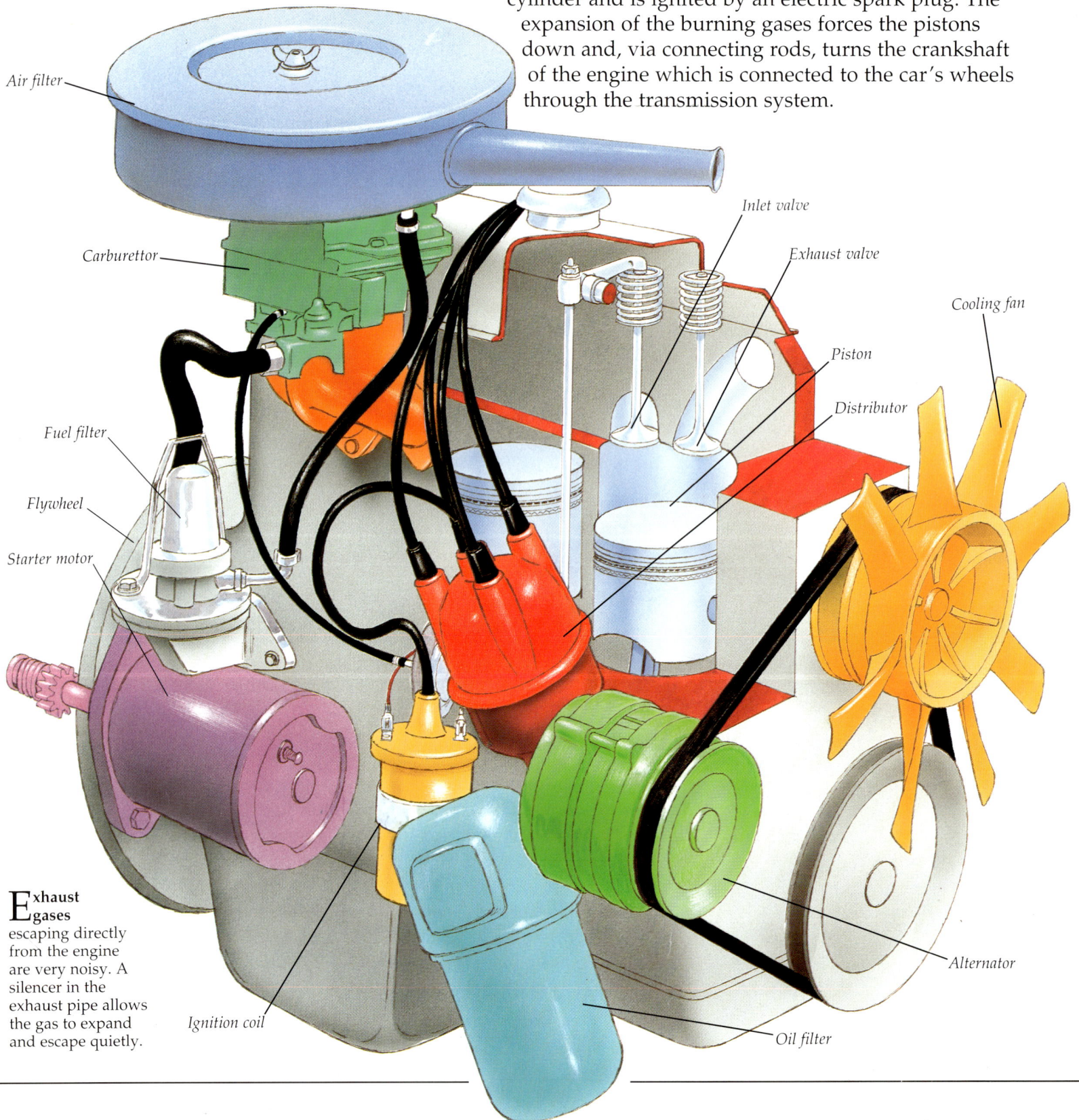

Air filter

Carburettor

Inlet valve

Exhaust valve

Cooling fan

Piston

Distributor

Fuel filter

Flywheel

Starter motor

Alternator

Exhaust **g**ases escaping directly from the engine are very noisy. A silencer in the exhaust pipe allows the gas to expand and escape quietly.

Ignition coil

Oil filter

Inlet valve *Exhaust valve* *Spark plug*

Induction stroke. The inlet valve opens and the piston moves down, drawing the petrol/air mixture into the cylinder.

Compression stroke. Both inlet and exhaust valves are closed, and the piston moves upwards, compressing the mixture.

Power stroke. The compressed mixture is ignited by the spark plug. The burning gases expand, pushing the piston down.

Exhaust stroke. The exhaust valve opens. The rising piston pushes the exhaust gases from the cylinder. The valve closes.

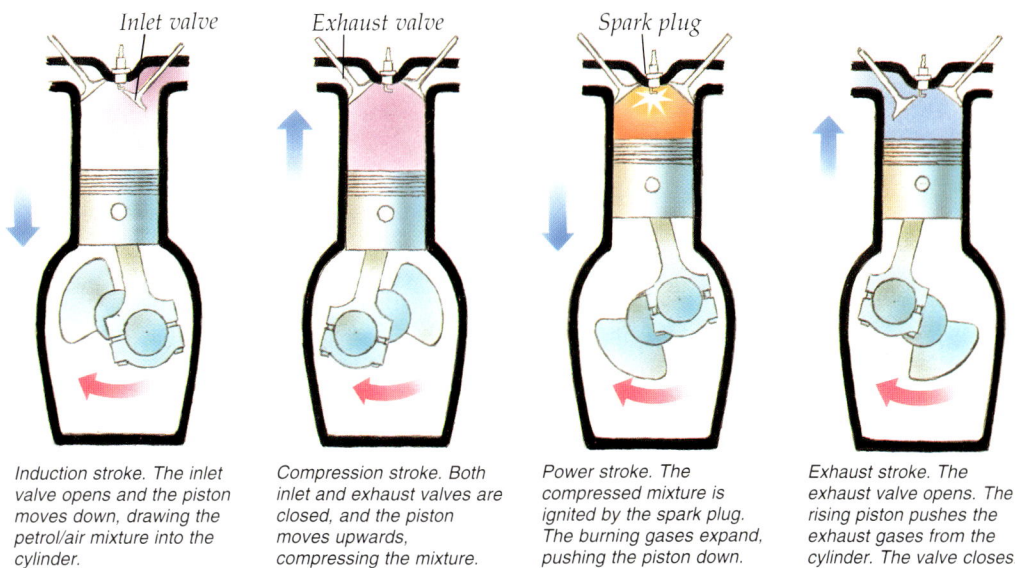

Most petrol engines work on the four-stroke cycle (*above*) developed in 1876 by the German engineer Nikolas Otto (1832-1891). Power is produced only on the third stroke of the cycle, so multi-cylindered engines are used to give a smooth power output. Diesel engines work on the same principle, but do not have spark plugs. The fuel is injected into the cylinders and ignited by the heating effect of the compression stroke. The engine gets very hot, so the cylinders are cooled to prevent overheating. Most cars have water cooling jackets around the cylinders and heat is lost through the radiator. A water-pump driven by the crankshaft circulates the cooling water. The crankshaft also drives a pump to force lubricating oil through the engine bearings, and an alternator to generate electricity in the car's electrical system.

Sensor *Sensor* *Sensor* *Alarm system and siren*

Concern for the environment is now important. Unleaded petrol, which must be used in cars with catalytic converters, has fewer harmful substances than old-style leaded petrol.

Many car alarms work by monitoring air movements within the car. Any movement triggers the alarm. Coded radio signals from a hand-held remote control unit turn the alarm on and off.

Remote control unit

AIR BAGS

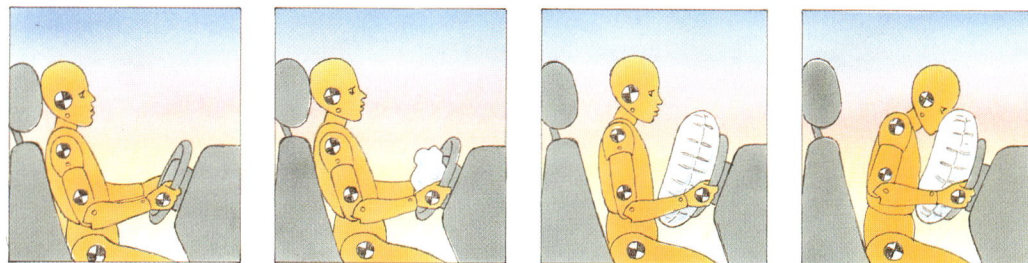

Air bags, which inflate in a crash to stop the driver's head hitting the steering wheel, are now fitted in many cars.

In a crash, a sensor detects rapid deceleration and triggers the air bag's inflation from the steering wheel.

Four-hundredths of a second after impact, the air bag has been fully inflated by a small cylinder of compressed gas.

One-hundredth of a second later, the driver's head hits the air bag, not the steering wheel.

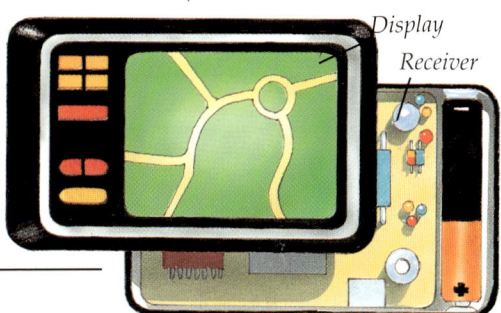

Display *Receiver*

Mounted on a car's dashboard, the Trafficmaster car computer picks up infrared signals from roadside transmitters which relay information about traffic conditions from a control centre. The receiver unit displays maps of the area and messages about hold-ups. The service is only available in a few urban areas and on some motorways.

FROM PETROL POWER TO SOLAR POWER

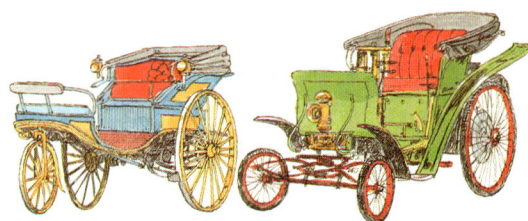

The Benz Tricycle of 1885 (left), an early petrol-engined car. By 1895, the basic front-engine and rear-wheel-drive, until recently used in most cars, had been pioneered by the French car-makers Panhard and Levassor (right).

In 1908, the American engineer Henry Ford (1863-1947) designed the Model T Ford to be easy to drive and repair. Mass-production reduced prices, so cars were no longer luxuries.[1] Over 15 million were made between 1908 and 1927.

The Volkswagen ('People's Car') Beetle was designed on the orders of Adolf Hitler in 1934. By 1990 over 21 million had been made - more than any other car. It was designed by Dr. Ferry Porsche, better known for his sports cars.

The British engineer Alec Issigonis (1906-1988) designed the Morris Minor in 1948. It remained in production until 1970. He also designed the Mini. Introduced in 1959, its front-wheel drive and combined engine/gearbox unit was revolutionary.

Since this 1960s Datsun went on sale, Japanese cars have become increasingly popular. Advanced manufacturing techniques, improved designs and good value make them serious rivals to European and American car makers.

Solar-powered vehicles may one day provide a pollution-free alternative to the internal combustion engine.

17

The American inventor Thomas Alva Edison (1847-1931) played a leading role in the invention of the light bulb and pioneered electrical power systems.

The American scientist Benjamin Franklin (1706-1790) flew a kite in a thunderstorm to show that lightning flashes were huge electric sparks. DO NOT TRY THIS YOURSELF!

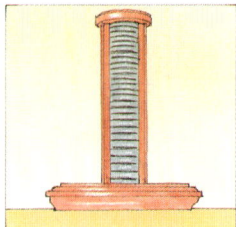

The work of Luigi Galvani (1737-1798), an Italian professor of anatomy, led to the discovery that muscles are controlled by electric currents.

The Italian scientist Alessandro Volta (1745-1827) made the first electric battery, the Voltaic pile, in 1800. The electrical unit, the Volt, is named after him.

As well as his work on electricity, Michael Faraday (1791-1867) made improved types of steel, and helped develop electric lighting for lighthouses.

Hippolyte Pixii, a French instrument maker, made the first modern electric generator in 1832.. All modern power station generators are based on it.

LIGHT AND POWER
ELECTRICITY

IMAGINE LIFE WITHOUT ELECTRICITY: no radio, telephone, television, video, electric lighting or heating. There would be no electric trains, underground or overground, to take people to work. Petrol-driven vehicles need electricity for their ignition systems, so there might be less traffic!

The scientific study of electricity began in the 18th century. The first electric battery, the Voltaic pile, was invented in 1800. In 1821 the English scientist Michael Faraday built the first electric motor, and in 1831 he made the scientific discoveries that led to the development of electric generators and power transmission systems. Electricity was first used for communications in the 1830s, in battery-powered electric telegraphs (page 29).

The development, in the 1870s, of the incandescent lamp (electric light bulb) for house lighting led to the building of power stations in towns and cities to light the houses of the wealthy. Electric trams and trains were developed in the 1880s.

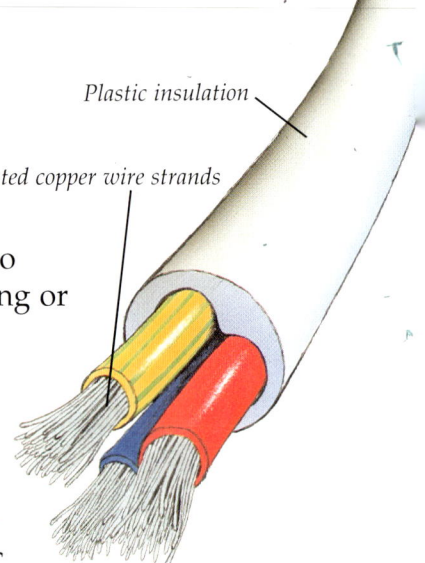

German plug and socket

Most plugs and sockets join three pairs of wires together. Two pairs (the live and neutral ones) are connected to the electricity supply; the third (the earth) is connected to the ground, ensuring that the outside of the gadget cannot cause electric shocks.

American plug and socket

Electricity is useful but dangerous. Plugs and sockets are used to connect the electrical gadgets safely into the electrical power supply. Different countries have different designs of plugs and sockets. Remember – NEVER TRY TO TAKE ANY ELECTRICAL GADGET, PLUG OR SOCKET APART!

French plug and socket

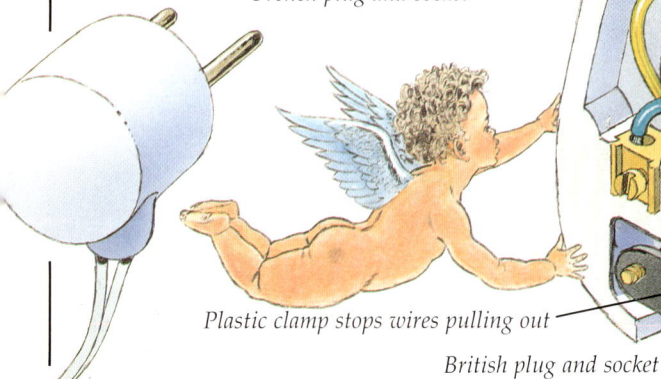

Plastic insulation

Twisted copper wire strands

Within the outer plastic layer of most electric flex are three bundles of twisted copper wires, covered with plastic insulation colour-coded for live, neutral and earth. The colour codes vary between countries.

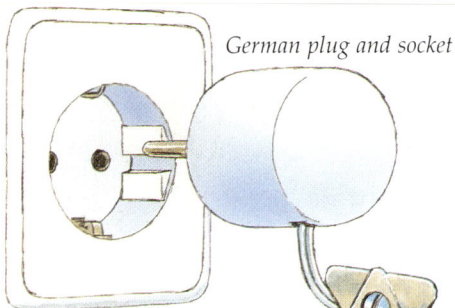

The British standard plug contains a fuse which, if the gadget is overloaded, breaks the electric circuit. A plastic clamp stops the wires pulling out of the plug. Shutters in the socket cover the live and neutral terminals.

On/off switch

Plastic clamp stops wires pulling out

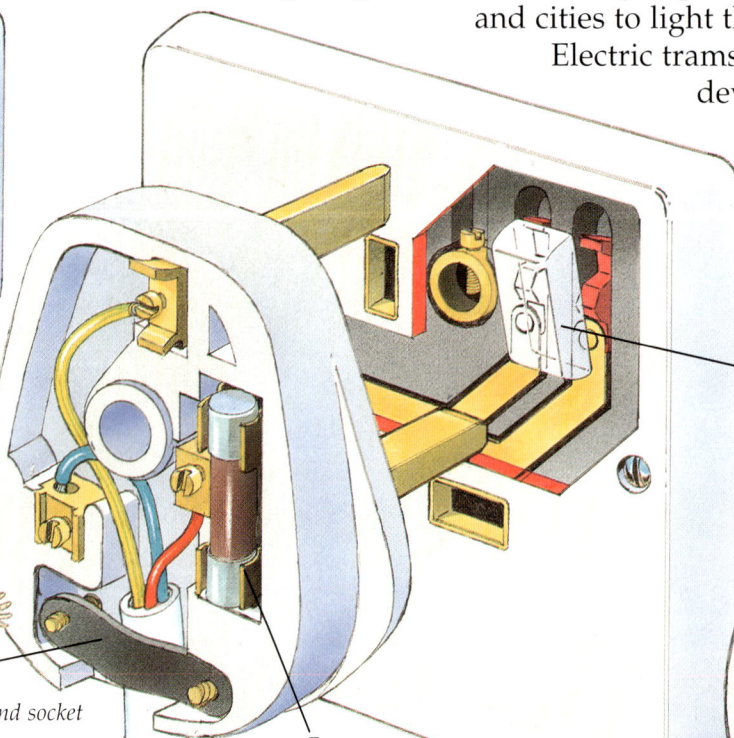

British plug and socket

Fuse

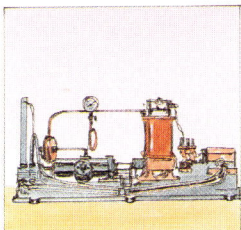

In 1884 the British engineer Sir Charles Parsons (1854-1931) built the first steam turbine generators. All coal, oil and nuclear power stations now use turbines.

Deptford Power Station in London, England, designed by the British engineer Sebastian de Ferranti (1864-1930), was the first large-scale power station.

Electric trains were introduced in the 1880s in America, Britain and Germany. The first electric tube railway was built in London in 1890.

Pylons carrying power lines are a familiar sight. The first long-distance power systems were built in Germany and America in the 1890s.

Nuclear power stations have generated electricity since the 1950s. But accidents and concern over radioactive waste and pollution make them unpopular.

Wind farms use giant windmills to generate electricity, but can only provide a fraction of our needs. They are also noisy and spoil landscapes.

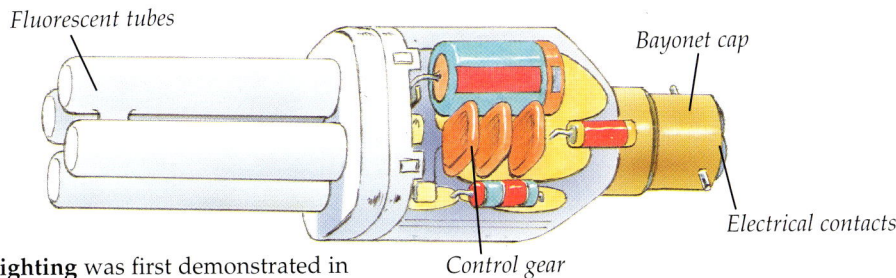

Fluorescent tubes

Bayonet cap

Electrical contacts

Control gear

Fluorescent tubes are four to five times more efficient than ordinary light bulbs because they do not waste so much energy in heat. The energy-efficient light bulb is really a folded fluorescent tube roughly the same size as an ordinary light bulb, and fitting into the same type of socket.

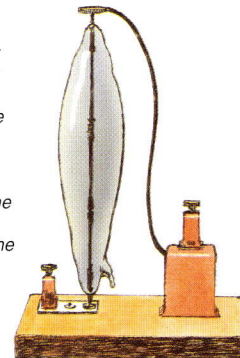

Electric lighting was first demonstrated in 1805, by the British scientist Sir Humphry Davy (1778-1829). It was used first in lighthouses from the 1850s. However, these arc lights were suitable only for outdoor use or in very large buildings, like railway stations and factories. Electric lighting for homes became possible when the incandescent electric lamp (light bulb) was invented in 1878-79. Light bulbs were being mass-produced by the mid-1880s, but domestic electric lighting remained a luxury until the 1930s. Fluorescent lights were introduced in 1939, but only for industrial and office buildings. The glass tube of a fluorescent lamp glows when electricity is passed through the gas (usually mercury vapour) inside.

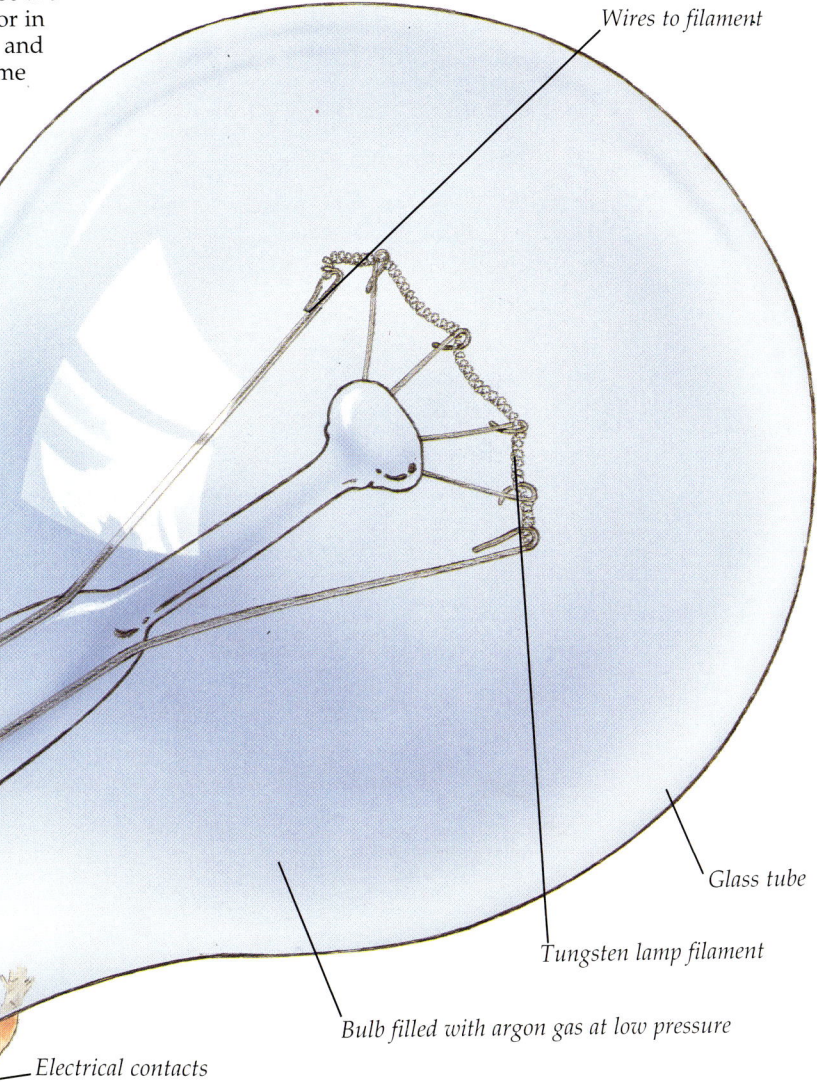

In Britain the chemist Sir Joseph Swan (1828-1914) is credited with the invention of the light bulb. His first bulb was shown in January 1879.

Wires to filament

In the USA Thomas Alva Edison (1847-1931) is regarded as the inventor of the light bulb. His first successful bulb was patented in October 1879.

Glass tube

Tungsten lamp filament

Bulb filled with argon gas at low pressure

Electrical contacts

The coiled tungsten filament in a light bulb glows white-hot when an electric current passes through it. The first light bulbs had carbon filaments.

Tungsten filaments were invented in 1908. To stop them burning up in the heat, oxygen is excluded by filling bulbs with argon gas at low pressure.

The filaments are coils of coiled wire. Coiling the wire means the filament can be very long, so the bulb shines brighter and lasts longer.

Edison's bulbs had better filaments. Swan's way of extracting air from bulbs was more efficient. In 1883, in Britain, they started making bulbs like these.

LIGHT AND POWER
SUPPLYING POWER

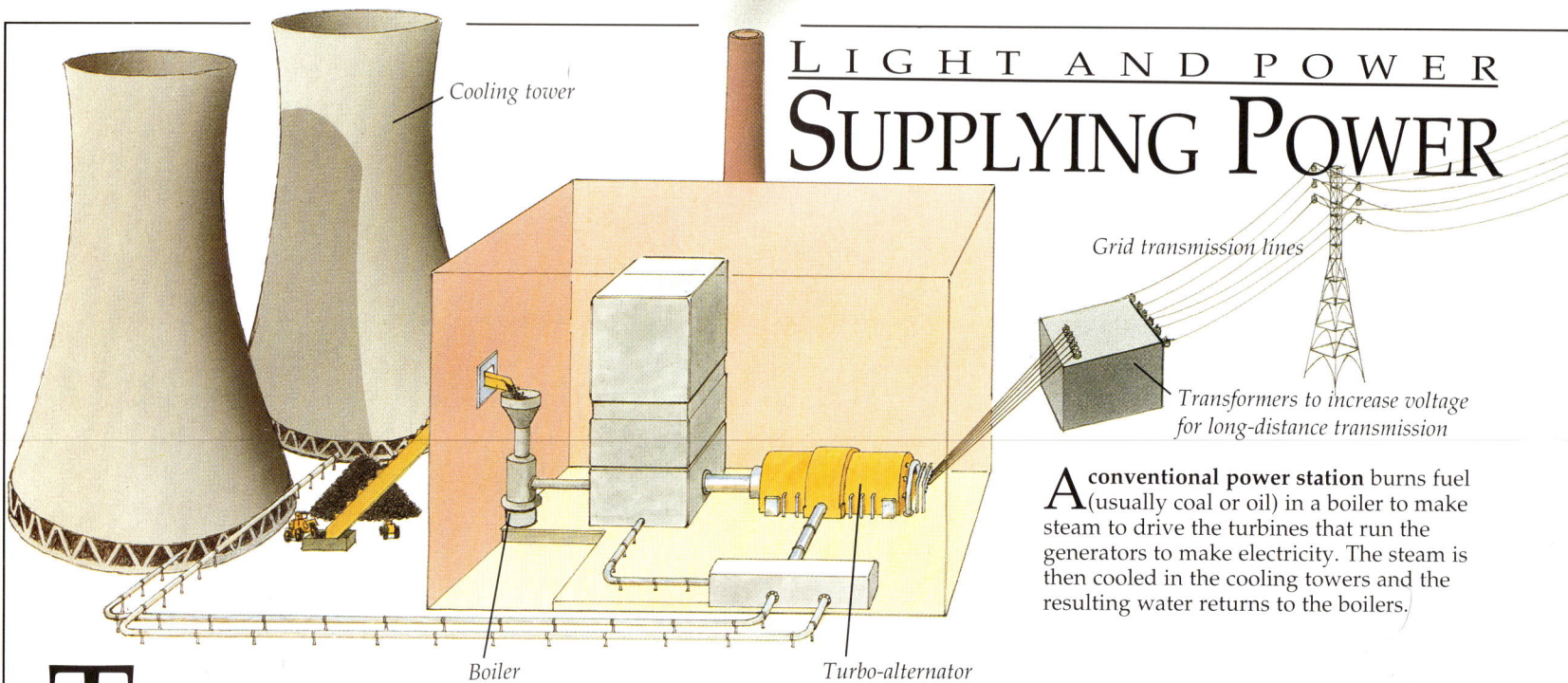

Cooling tower

Grid transmission lines

Transformers to increase voltage for long-distance transmission

A **conventional power station** burns fuel (usually coal or oil) in a boiler to make steam to drive the turbines that run the generators to make electricity. The steam is then cooled in the cooling towers and the resulting water returns to the boilers.

Boiler

Turbo-alternator

THE KEY FEATURES OF POWER SUPPLY SYSTEMS are easy to spot: large power stations, often with prominent cooling towers, electricity pylons marching across the landscape and groups of transformers at electricity sub-stations. In towns electricity for homes usually passes along underground cables. When it reaches houses or flats, the electricity passes first through fuses or circuit breakers. These will cut off the power if there is an electrical overload. The electricity then passes through a meter, which measures how much is used, so electricity companies know what to charge for the power used. Inside the home are different electric circuits: wall sockets for powering domestic appliances and lighting are the most obvious. Electric cookers, which use lots of power, and some water heaters have their own circuits.

In this American house the water heater, clothes drier, washing machine and cooker (which all use lots of electricity) each have their own 240V circuit. Each floor has its own 120V power and lighting circuit. All the cables are connected to the main electricity supply at the circuit box. In Britain, lighting and power circuits are separate and both are 240V.

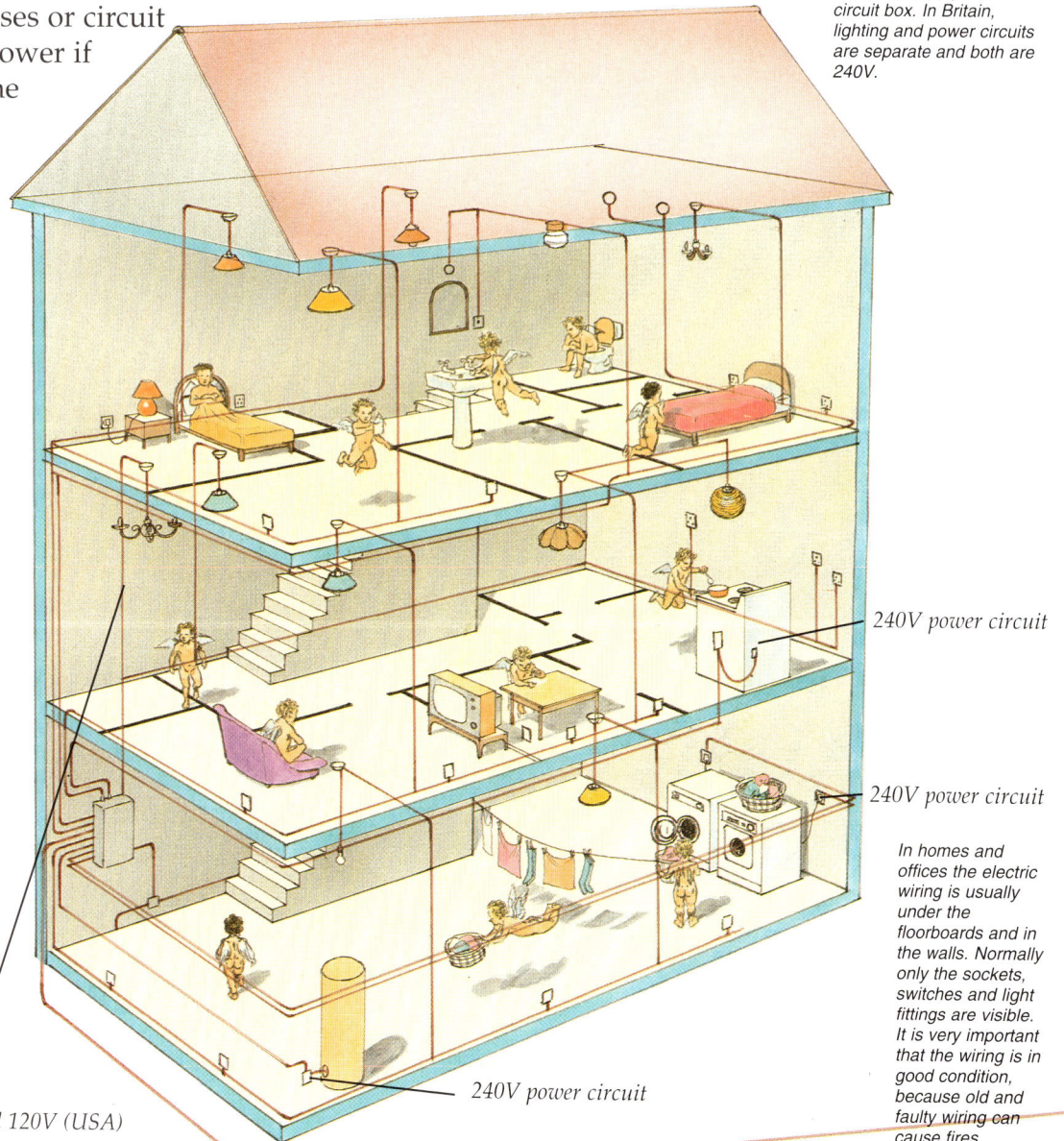

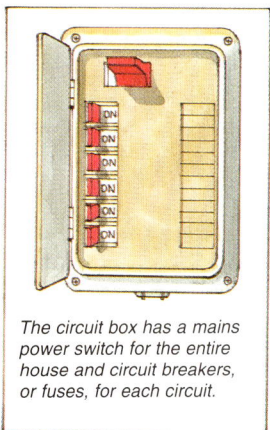

240V power circuit

240V power circuit

In homes and offices the electric wiring is usually under the floorboards and in the walls. Normally only the sockets, switches and light fittings are visible. It is very important that the wiring is in good condition, because old and faulty wiring can cause fires.

The circuit box has a mains power switch for the entire house and circuit breakers, or fuses, for each circuit.

240V power circuit

240V (UK) or 240V and 120V (USA)

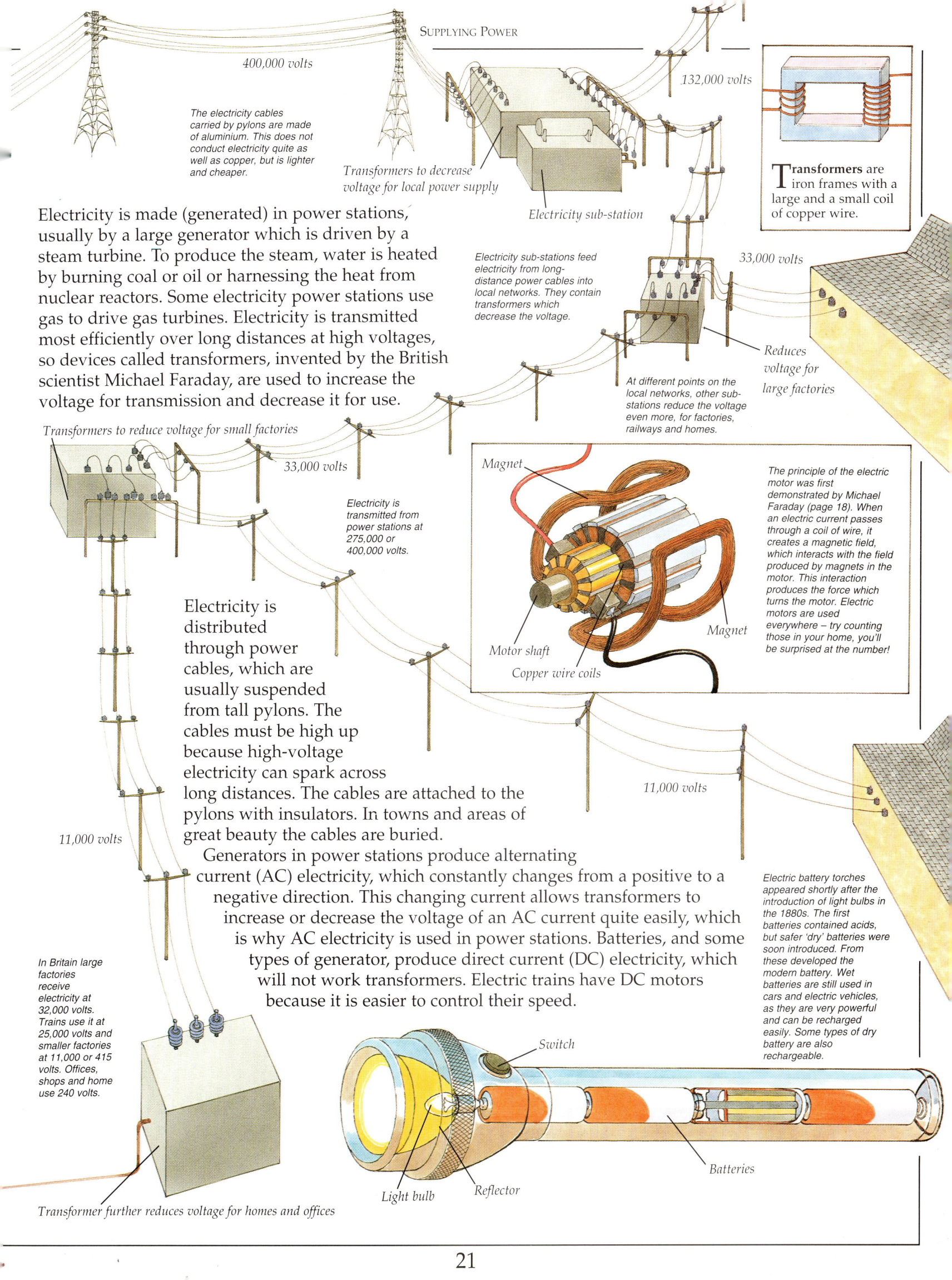

400,000 volts

The electricity cables carried by pylons are made of aluminium. This does not conduct electricity quite as well as copper, but is lighter and cheaper.

Transformers to decrease voltage for local power supply

Electricity sub-station

132,000 volts

Transformers are iron frames with a large and a small coil of copper wire.

Electricity is made (generated) in power stations, usually by a large generator which is driven by a steam turbine. To produce the steam, water is heated by burning coal or oil or harnessing the heat from nuclear reactors. Some electricity power stations use gas to drive gas turbines. Electricity is transmitted most efficiently over long distances at high voltages, so devices called transformers, invented by the British scientist Michael Faraday, are used to increase the voltage for transmission and decrease it for use.

Electricity sub-stations feed electricity from long-distance power cables into local networks. They contain transformers which decrease the voltage.

33,000 volts

Reduces voltage for large factories

Transformers to reduce voltage for small factories

33,000 volts

Electricity is transmitted from power stations at 275,000 or 400,000 volts.

At different points on the local networks, other sub-stations reduce the voltage even more, for factories, railways and homes.

Magnet

The principle of the electric motor was first demonstrated by Michael Faraday (page 18). When an electric current passes through a coil of wire, it creates a magnetic field, which interacts with the field produced by magnets in the motor. This interaction produces the force which turns the motor. Electric motors are used everywhere – try counting those in your home, you'll be surprised at the number!

Magnet

Motor shaft

Copper wire coils

Electricity is distributed through power cables, which are usually suspended from tall pylons. The cables must be high up because high-voltage electricity can spark across long distances. The cables are attached to the pylons with insulators. In towns and areas of great beauty the cables are buried.

Generators in power stations produce alternating current (AC) electricity, which constantly changes from a positive to a negative direction. This changing current allows transformers to increase or decrease the voltage of an AC current quite easily, which is why AC electricity is used in power stations. Batteries, and some types of generator, produce direct current (DC) electricity, which will not work transformers. Electric trains have DC motors because it is easier to control their speed.

11,000 volts

11,000 volts

In Britain large factories receive electricity at 32,000 volts. Trains use it at 25,000 volts and smaller factories at 11,000 or 415 volts. Offices, shops and home use 240 volts.

Electric battery torches appeared shortly after the introduction of light bulbs in the 1880s. The first batteries contained acids, but safer 'dry' batteries were soon introduced. From these developed the modern battery. Wet batteries are still used in cars and electric vehicles, as they are very powerful and can be recharged easily. Some types of dry battery are also rechargeable.

Switch

Transformer further reduces voltage for homes and offices

Light bulb

Reflector

Batteries

HOW THE SLR WORKS

Before the shutter release button is pressed, the shutter is closed and the mirror is down, so you can see what you will photograph.

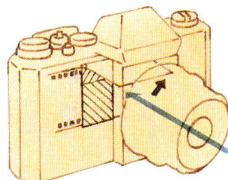

When the button is pressed, the mirror moves up so that light can reach the film when the shutter opens.

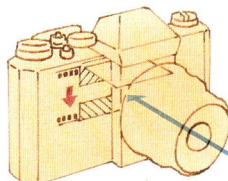

The shutter consists of two overlapping blinds. The first covers the film. It moves down, exposing the film after the mirror flips up.

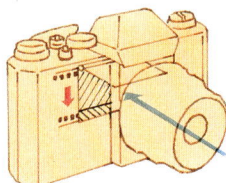

The second blind then moves down, covering the film again. The exposure, the time between the blinds exposing and covering the film, can be varied.

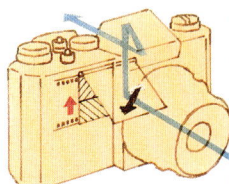

Then the mirror drops down again, so the viewfinder can be used once more. The film is moved on and the shutter reset.

TAKING PICTURES
THE SLR CAMERA

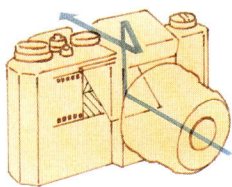

A REFLEX CAMERA has a viewfinder which shows the picture formed by the camera's lens, making it easier to focus the lens and aim the camera.

Simpler cameras have lenses which do not need focusing and viewfinders which only help aim the camera. The first reflex camera, the twin-lens, used two identical lenses, one for the picture and one for the viewfinder. These cameras were quite large and bulky. In the 1930s the smaller single-lens reflex (SLR) camera was developed. A hinged mirror, which moves out of the way when the photograph is taken, reflects light into a five-faced prism (the pentaprism), which gives the image in the viewfinder.

The term '35mm' refers to a width of film. It is the standard cine camera film. In 1913 Oskar Barnack, an engineer with the German camera-maker Leitz, made the first 35mm 'still' camera, primarily to use cine film offcuts. Cameras using 35mm film could be much smaller than those which used roll film 120mm wide. As a result, in 1925 Leitz began making high-quality 'Leica' 35mm 'miniature' cameras, which were about the same size as a modern 35mm SLR camera.

A modern 35mm SLR, like this one, has sophisticated electronic control systems to give the correct exposure, and can focus the lens automatically.

The first cameras took photographs on metal plates coated with light-sensitive material. Photographic glass plates followed in 1851 and paper roll film was introduced in the 1880s. Then, in 1889, George Eastman (1854-1932) introduced celluloid (an early plastic) film.

The modern 35mm SLR camera is small, light and easy to use. Many early cameras were too heavy to carry around easily.

Shutter release button

Electronic exposure control silicon chip

Film transport mechanism

Film sprocket

35mm film

Batteries

The 35mm film comes in a light-tight cassette, with a leader strip sticking out to feed into the film transport mechanism. The film has a series of rectangular holes along both edges. Teeth in the film transport mechanism engage these holes and pull the film along between each exposure. After all the film has been exposed, it is wound back into the cassette, and can then be removed and sent for processing.

Cameras have mechanical or electronic systems to move the film on between photographs and to work the shutter to expose the film and control the amount of light falling on the film. Controlling the light depends on the shutter speed, the opening of the iris diaphragm in the lens, the sensitivity of the film and the amount of light on the object being photographed.

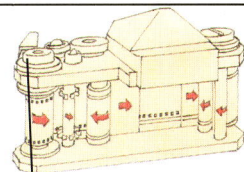

The camera lens is made up of a number of different elements designed to produce an accurate image on the film. Inside the lens is the metal iris diaphragm which controls the amount of light coming through the lens, and so the brightness of the image. The lenses are interchangeable; they can be changed quickly for close-up, wide-angle or telephoto shots.

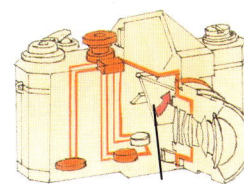

Film wind lever

Moving the film-wind lever resets the shutter for the next photograph, as well as moving the film along.

Mirror

The through-the-lens metering system shows exactly how much light will fall on the film when the shutter opens.

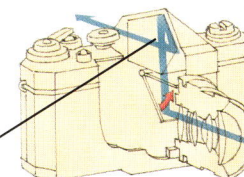

Pentaprism

The path light follows through the SLR camera to reach the viewfinder.

Colour negatives

Slot for flash gun

Mirror

Iris diaphragm

Lens elements

TAKING PICTURES
INSTANT PHOTOGRAPHS

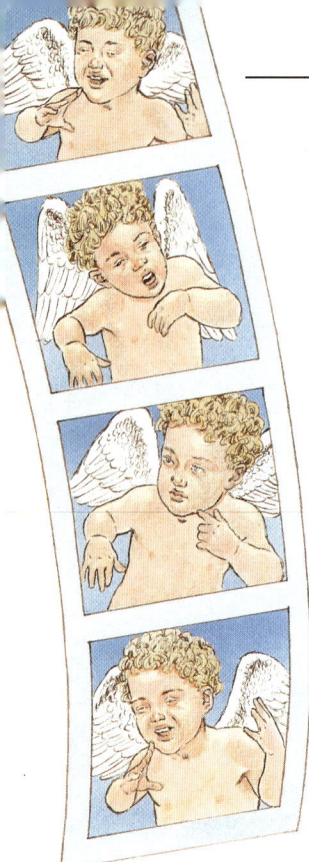

TAKING PHOTOGRAPHS has always involved two messy and time-consuming processes called 'developing' and 'printing'. At first, photographers had to do the developing and printing themselves. Then, in 1888, an American, George Eastman, designed a simple, foolproof camera, which used another new invention - film on a roll.

Photographers took their photographs, returned the camera to Eastman's factory and it came back with a new film in place and a set of finished photographs. The cameras soon became even easier to use and photographers loaded and unloaded the films themselves. Even today, everyone except photographic enthusiasts sends or takes film to be processed.

Film processing involves taking the exposed film from its container and treating it with chemicals in a light-proof box to make a picture you can see. All this is done automatically by machines. High-street photo shops have small machines called 'minilabs' to carry out processing on the spot. This is far quicker than sending the film to a specialist processing company. But the only way to get truly instant photographs is to combine the camera and the film processing machine. That is the system used by Polaroid cameras and the photo booths in stations and department stores which give you colour prints in minutes.

Minilab photographic printers: negatives are put in on the left and projected onto a strip of photographic paper. This is passed through developing chemicals and sliced up into individual photos which appear in the trays on the right.

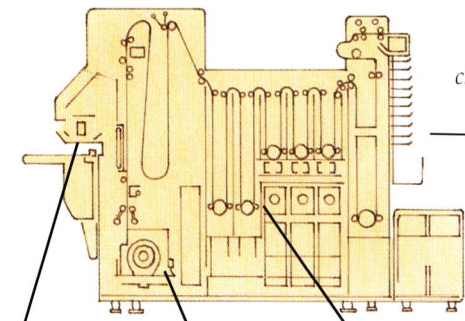

Reel of photographic paper

Camera

Rotating paper carriers

Paper drying rollers

Developing tank

Heater to keep developing chemicals at correct temperature

Trays for finished prints

Negative carrier

Reel of paper

Developing tanks

Electric motor driving paper carriers

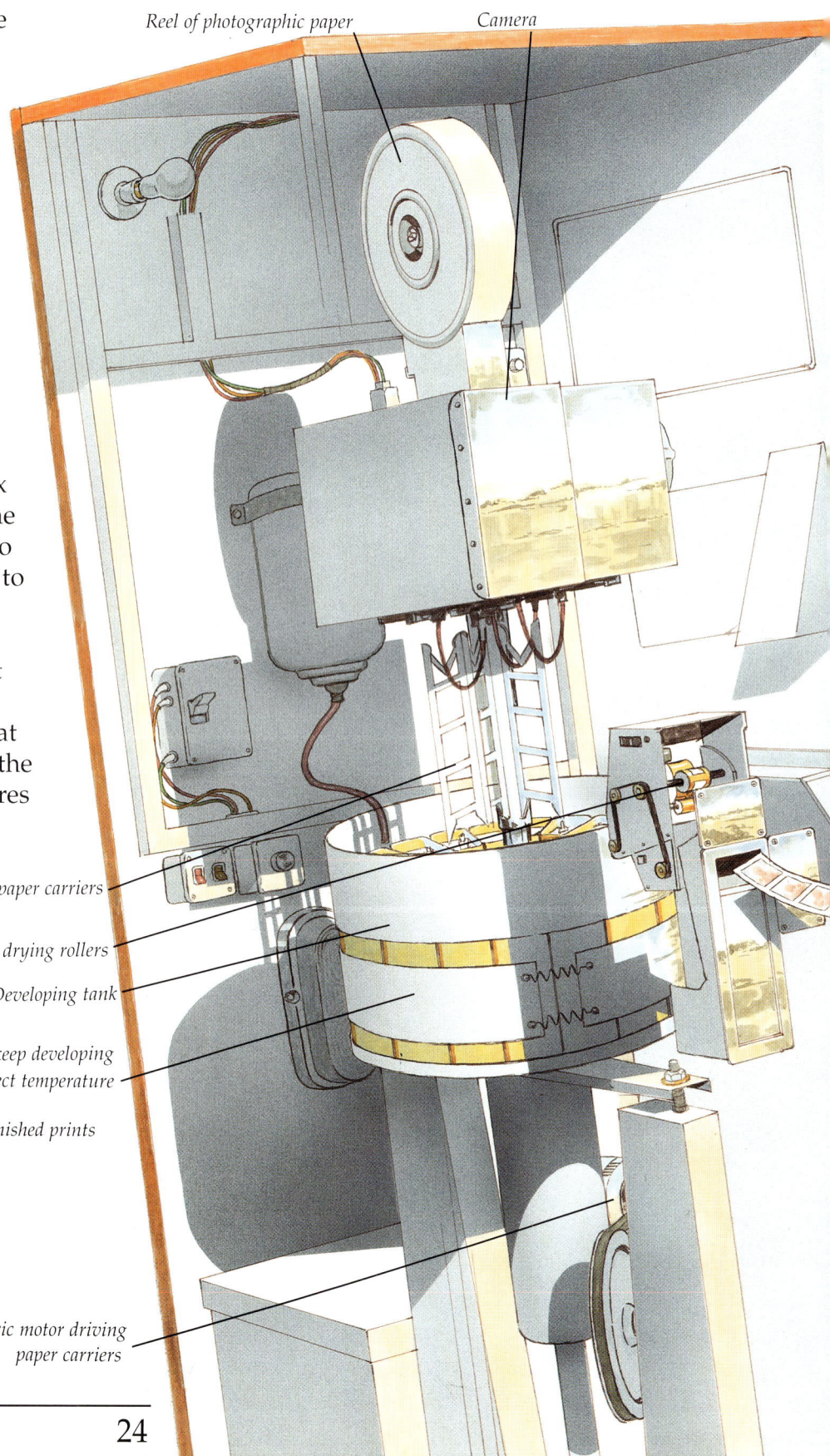

In the photo booth

Make the seat the right height, put in the money. Smile! The automatic camera inside takes a series of flash photographs.

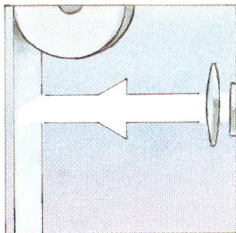

Instead of film, the camera uses a reel of photographic paper, which is moved automatically between photographs.

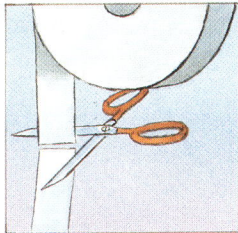

The exposed paper moves down between photographs and, after the fourth, it is cut and fed into a paper carrier.

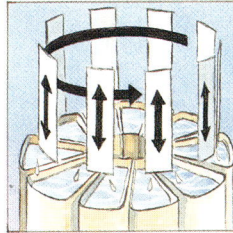

The paper carrier moves down, up and round, dunking the photographic strip in a series of developing tanks.

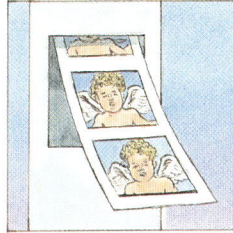

The developed strip is partly dried by fans, and ejected through drying rollers into a slot outside the booth for you to collect.

Thousands of photo booths are in use throughout the world – over 500,000 photographs are taken every day!

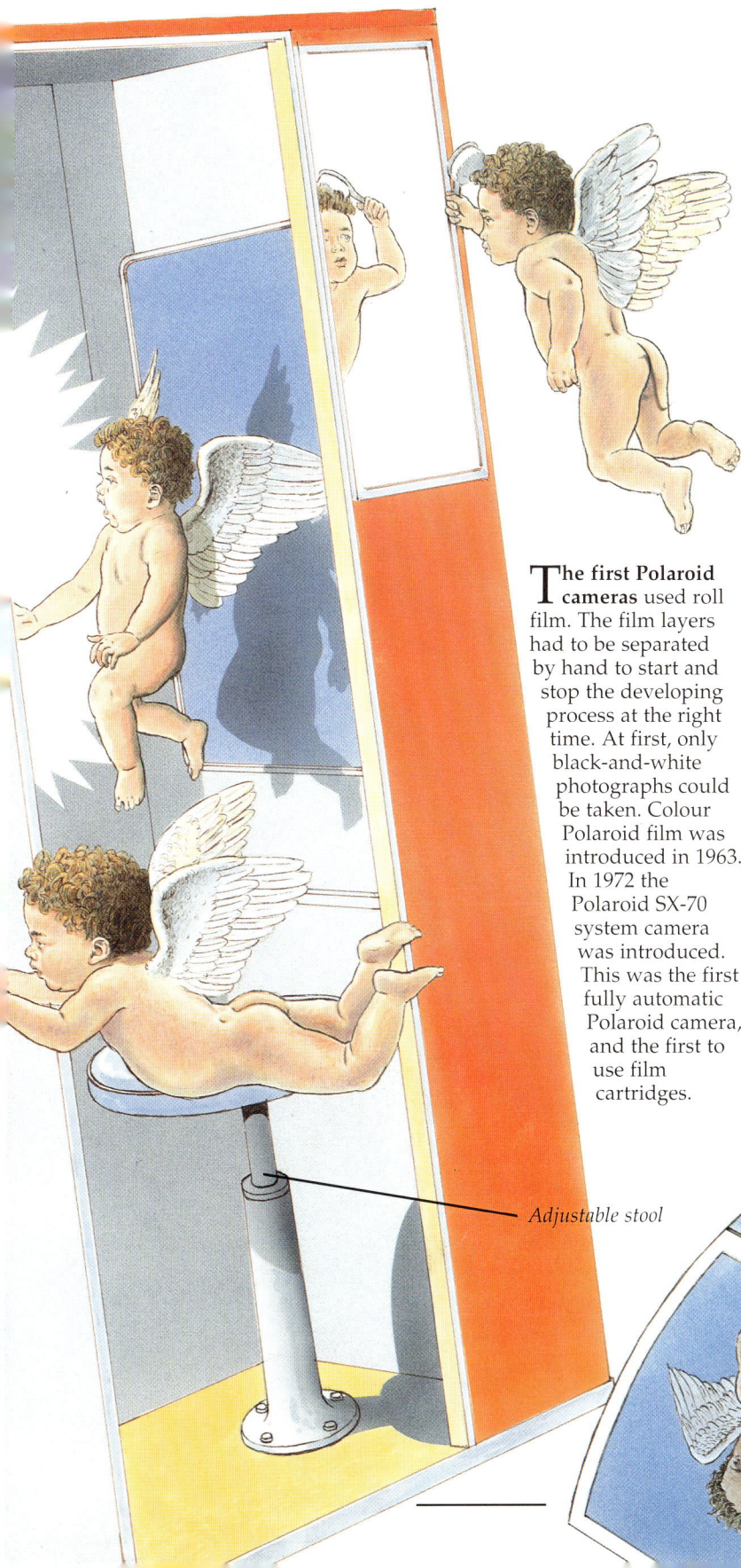

In 1947 an American inventor, Edwin Land (1909-1991), developed the Polaroid camera, which produces photographs only a minute after taking them. The Polaroid camera uses special film which develops itself. Instead of a roll of film, the camera is loaded with a cartridge containing a number of film packs - one per photograph. These packs contain both film and processing chemicals inside a sealed pod surrounding the film area. After the film has been exposed it is ejected through rollers which squeeze it, breaking the pod and spreading the processing chemicals over the film inside the pack to start the developing process. Unlike other types of film, Polaroid film develops itself in daylight.

The disadvantage of the Polaroid camera and the photo booth is that the photographs they produce are not from negatives, and so they cannot easily be copied or enlarged. Most cameras use negative film, which provides transparent pictures (negatives) with the light and dark areas transposed (the opposite way to how we see them). Photographs are printed from the negatives. This process means you can make any number of prints, and also make them larger or smaller than the negative if you want.

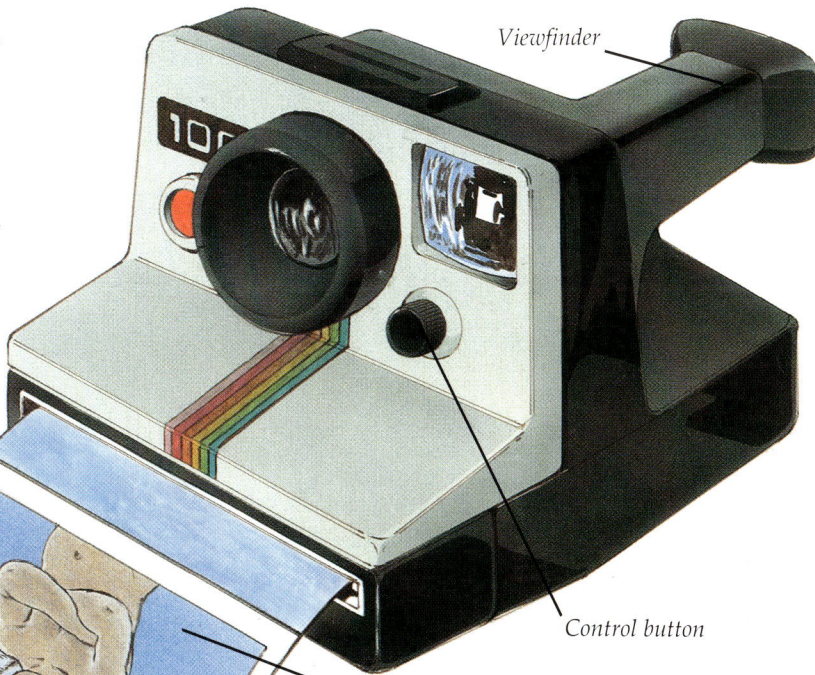

The first Polaroid cameras used roll film. The film layers had to be separated by hand to start and stop the developing process at the right time. At first, only black-and-white photographs could be taken. Colour Polaroid film was introduced in 1963. In 1972 the Polaroid SX-70 system camera was introduced. This was the first fully automatic Polaroid camera, and the first to use film cartridges.

Adjustable stool

Viewfinder

Control button

The result!

WORLDWIDE COMMUNICATIONS
TELEPHONE

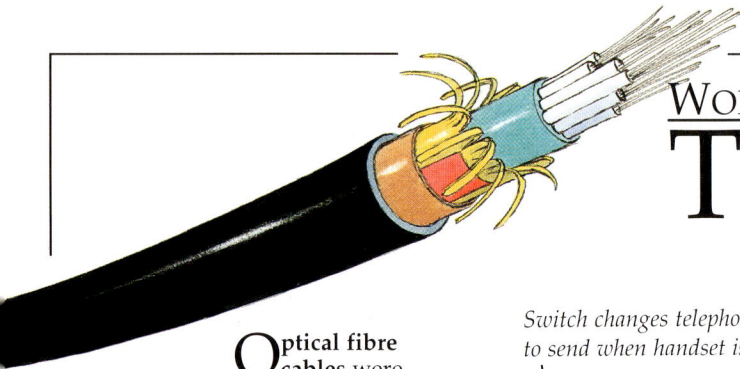

Optical fibre cables were introduced in the 1980s. The telephone signals are converted into coded pulses of laser light, which bounce down the cable's glass core. As well as being lighter and cheaper than ordinary wire cables, these can carry over ten times more phone calls and suffer no electrical interference.

Switch changes telephone from receive to send when handset is picked up

The **microphone** and loudspeaker in the handset (right) have changed little over the years, but the dialling keypad contains the latest silicon chip circuits.

A **tiny electric current** from the exchange passes through the mouthpiece when you pick up the phone. Speaking into the mouthpiece varies the current, producing a signal which is transmitted to the person you are calling via the telephone exchange. The electrical signals arriving at the other phone are converted back into sound by the earpiece. International calls may go through submarine cable links or via satellite.

Control circuits and microprocessor memory

Push buttons

Although born in Scotland, Alexander Graham Bell (1847-1922) became an American citizen. He taught deaf people to speak and his invention of the phone developed from this work.

To **ring a number**, press the buttons and silicon chip circuitry in the phone sends coded pulses to the telephone exchange, which connects you to the phone with that number.

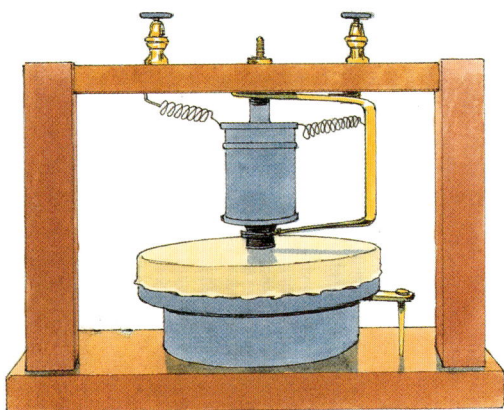

In 1875 Bell transmitted sounds, but not speech, using this 'Gallows' telephone. The sound waves vibrated a diaphragm similar to that in a modern telephone. Bell made his first successful telephone in 1876. He spoke through it to his assistant in the next room saying: 'Mr. Watson, come here I want to see you.'

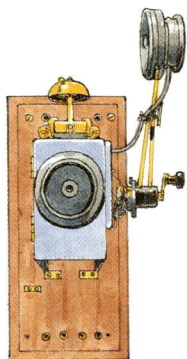

In 1877 the American inventor Thomas Alva Edison (1847-1931) invented the carbon microphone, which ensured the telephone's success.

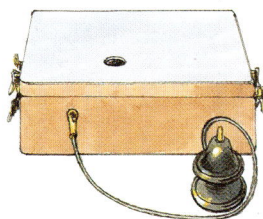

Edison also introduced separate mouthpieces for telephones. In the Crossley telephone, which he designed in 1880, the mouthpiece is in the box.

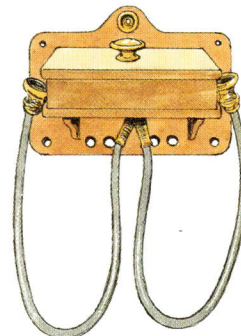

The Gower-Bell telephone of the early 1880s had a single mouthpiece and two listening tubes, so someone else could listen to the conversation.

By the 1890s the familiar style of handset began to emerge. Winding the handle of this ornate phone sent a signal to the operator at the exchange.

Earpiece

Electromagnet

Membrane

The earpiece contains an electromagnet, which vibrates a thin plastic membrane as the signal passes through it, producing sound. All loudspeakers work on this principle.

The familiar telephone handset consists of an earpiece and a mouthpiece. The earpiece is a small loudspeaker and the mouthpiece a small microphone. The telephone is connected by wires to the nearest exchange, which links callers together.

In 1962, the first telecommunications satellite Telstar-1 was launched. This could beam twelve telephone calls at a time between Europe and the USA. By 1969, the International Telecommunications Satellite organisation (Intelsat) had a network of orbiting satellites, providing a global telecommunications network capable of handling thousands of telephone, television and data signals simultaneously.

THE TELEPHONE, invented by Alexander Graham Bell in 1876, is the foundation of a world-wide communications network linking a quarter of the world's population. The telephone's basic technology has changed little since 1876, it is the changes to the telephone exchanges connecting individual lines that has made the communications revolution possible. At first, callers were connected manually by operators, but in 1889 Almon Strowger (1839-1902) invented the automatic telephone exchange, although these were not common until the 1920s. The coin-operated phone was also invented in 1889, by William Gray. In 1928 the first transatlantic telephone link was opened using radio. Undersea telephone cables connected England and France from 1891, but it was not until 1956 that the first telephone cable was laid across the Atlantic. It could carry only thirty-six calls at a time.

Membrane

Carbon granules

A membrane in the mouthpiece vibrates when you speak into it, compressing particles of carbon in the microphone. This varies the electric current passing through it from the exchange.

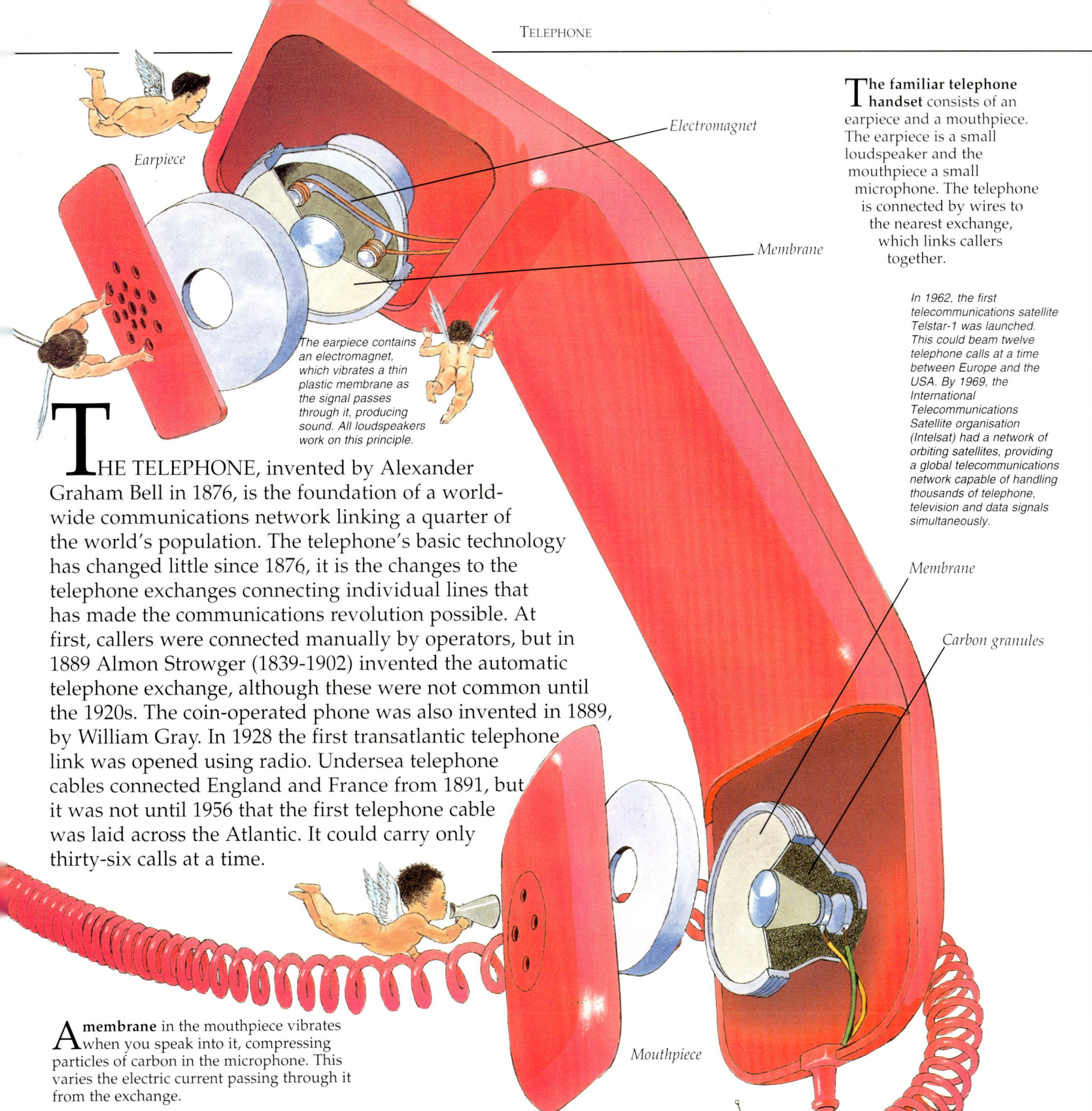

Mouthpiece

In this 'candlestick' telephone, which went on sale in 1905, lifting the receiver called the exchange, and replacing it disconnected the call.

The 1920s 'candlestick' phone incorporated a dial which could be used to call numbers via the automatic telephone exchanges that were coming into use.

By the 1930s most phone cases were plastic, and phone design changed little until push-button phones became common in the 1980s.

Modern telephones with fast and easy-to-use push-button 'dialling' have microprocessor memories which can store and re-dial numbers and divert calls.

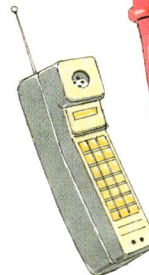

Portable phones became common in Europe in the 1980s, using cellular radio networks first used in the USA and Japan in the 1970s.

In the 1990s, the first practical videophones became available, so you could see as well as hear the person you were speaking to.

WORLDWIDE COMMUNICATIONS

THE FAX MACHINE

THE FACSIMILE MACHINE, better known as the fax, is now a vital office and business tool, enabling users to transmit drawings and all kinds of documents along telephone lines throughout the world. Without the international telecommunications network that developed with the telephone, fax machines would be much more limited in use. Although the first practical fax machine was built in 1865, faxes did not become common until the late 1970s when microprocessors, which could carry out the complex operation of converting the images into signals for transmission, became available. Before the days of the fax, messages were sent by teleprinter, machines rather like electric typewriters connected by phone and telegraph lines. You typed a message in, and it was printed by the machine at the other end of the line. The fax made these machines unnecessary.

By the 1970s, international standards for fax machines were set by the Comité Consultatif International Télégraphique et Téléphonique (CCITT), so that all fax machines could communicate with each other. Many fax machines now have a telephone and answering machine: three office tools in one. The text of this book went to and from author and editor by fax.

Fax machines can transmit a document like this page in roughly a minute. However, interference on the phone line can make parts of the page unreadable.

Feeder tray

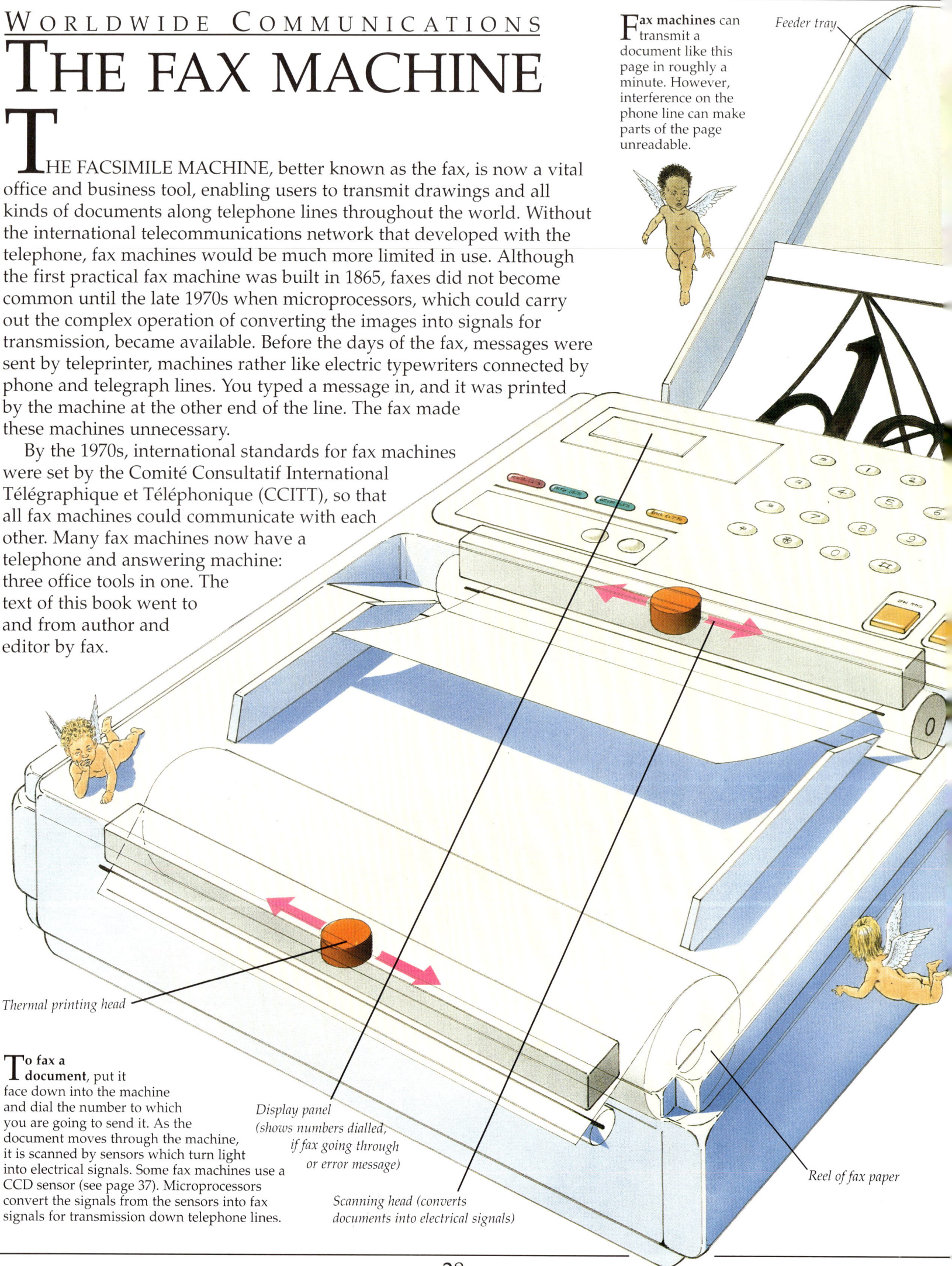

Thermal printing head

To fax a document, put it face down into the machine and dial the number to which you are going to send it. As the document moves through the machine, it is scanned by sensors which turn light into electrical signals. Some fax machines use a CCD sensor (see page 37). Microprocessors convert the signals from the sensors into fax signals for transmission down telephone lines.

Display panel (shows numbers dialled, if fax going through or error message)

Scanning head (converts documents into electrical signals)

Reel of fax paper

In England in the 1830s William Cooke and Charles Wheatstone both developed an electric telegraph. An American, Samuel Morse, also developed one. The telegraph inked messages in the dots and dashes of Morse code. The first message was 'What hath God wrought?' Morse sent it from Washington to Baltimore.

By 1900, electric telegraphs were sending messages across the world in a few hours, using land lines and undersea cables.

Teleprinters were a development of the 19th-century printing telegraphs. These printed the actual text of a message without using code. During the 1980s they were largely superseded by fax machines.

The Creed teleprinter of 1928 was used for all inland telegraph messages sent throughout the British Isles.

The Belinographe telephoto machine of 1925, one of the first successful fax machines, was used to transmit black-and-white photos by the telephone network.

Document being faxed

Before a fax is sent, the sending and receiving fax machines exchange 'handshake signals' to check that they can communicate with each other.

The first commercial fax service was started by the Italian scientist Giovanni Caselli (1815-1891) in 1865. The first fax machine had been built in 1843 by the Scottish inventor Alexander Bain (1818-1903), but he did not develop his invention.

Microprocessor to produce fax signals

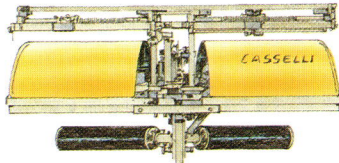

Message **and portrait** of Caselli (*top*) faxed by his machines. Messages were written on a curved metal plate in special ink which did not conduct electricity. The plate was scanned by a moving needle through which electricity passed except where the message interrupted the current. The message was reproduced on electrically sensitive paper. Caselli set up his machines in Paris and Lyon, France, in 1865.

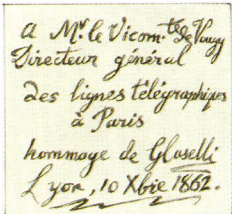

Incoming document

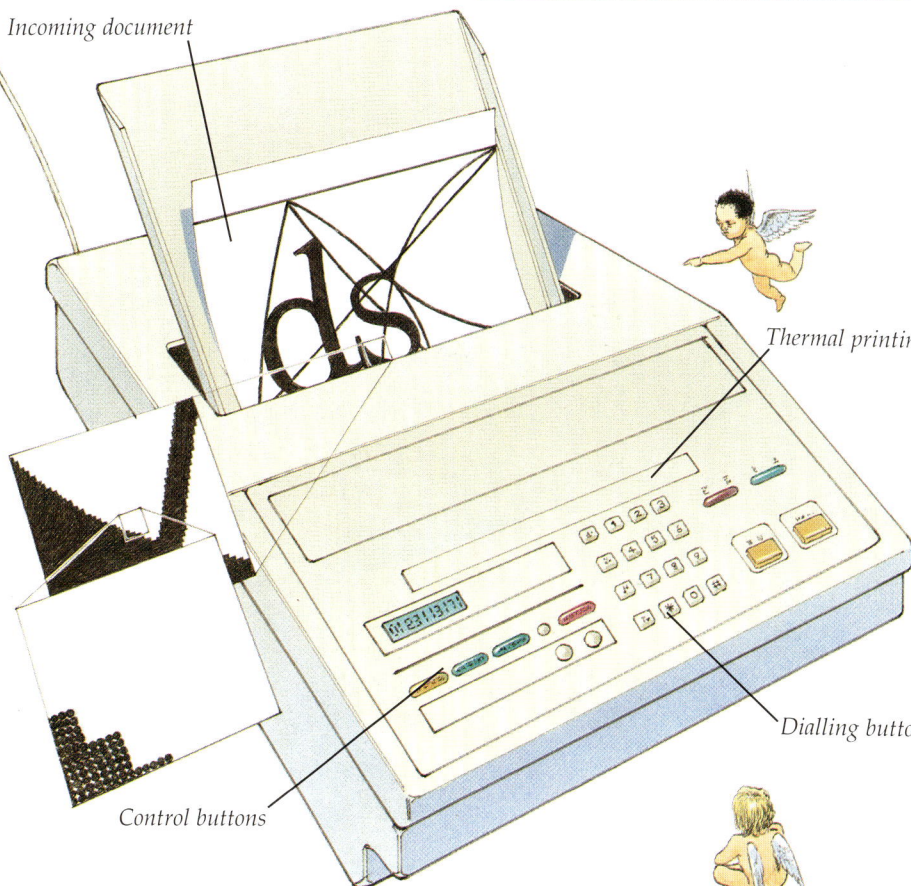

Thermal printing head

Dialling buttons

Control buttons

The receiving fax machine converts incoming signals into instructions to the thermal head to print the document as a series of tiny dots on special fax paper.

LISTENING IN
RADIO

An early transistor radio made by PYE in 1959.

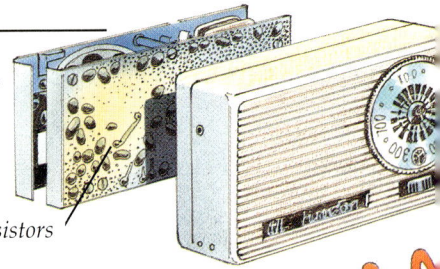

Circuit board with transistors

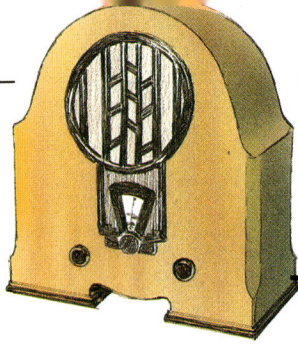

RADIO WAS FIRST USED FOR COMMUNICATION in 1896, by the Italian scientist Guglielmo Marconi. He developed the research into electromagnetic radiation of the Scottish physicist James Clerk Maxwell (1831-1879) and the German physicist Heinrich Hertz (1857-1894). Hertz had demonstrated the existence of the form of electromagnetic radiation we call radio waves. The frequency of radio waves' vibrations is measured in Hertz – 1Hz = 1 oscillation per second.

At first, radio messages could be transmitted only in the dot-dash signals of Morse code, using buzzers developed for electric telegraph systems (see page 29). Then, in 1906, the Canadian engineer Reginald Fessenden (1866-1932) transmitted sound by radio experimentally. However, it was the development of the thermionic valve by John Ambrose Fleming (1849-1945) in Britain in 1904 and Lee de Forest (1873-1961) in America from 1906 that made transmitting sound easy.

Circuit board containing tuning and amplifier circuits

Ferrite bar aerial

Rod aerial

Batteries

Integrated circuit – makes small radios possible

Loudspeaker

Radios became smaller and more sensitive as scientists and engineers learnt more about transmitting sound. This Philips 'Superinductance' radio of 1933 did not need a large outdoor aerial as earlier radios had.

The electromagnetic spectrum consists of many types of electromagnetic radiation, Radio waves are one of them. All travel at the speed of light: 300,000 km per second.

Morse code, developed for electric telegraph systems by the American inventor Samuel Morse (1791-1872), was first used in 1838. It was also used for the earliest radio messages.

The Scottish physicist James Clerk Maxwell (1831-1879) predicted the existence of electromagnetic radiation. His theories, called Maxwell's Laws, describe how the radiation travels.

In 1887-88, the German physicist Heinrich Hertz (1857-1894) proved that Maxwell was correct. Using a primitive radio transmitter and receiver, he showed that electromagnetic waves existed.

Guglielmo Marconi (1874-1937), the radio pioneer, was inspired by Hertz's work. In 1901 he sent a radio signal from Poldhu in Cornwall, England, to St John's in Newfoundland, Canada.

Radio signals can be used for remote-control model cars and aircraft. However, if several are operated together, each must use a different frequency.

The frequencies used by radio and television stations are agreed internationally. AM signals use long and medium wavebands and FM signals use VHF wavebands.

Television signals are transmitted on the UHF (Ultra High Frequency) radio waveband. The television tube converts the television signals into a picture.

The first experimental radio broadcasts for public entertainment were made in 1920 by British and American radio companies.

Liquid Crystal Display

The transistor, invented in 1947, superseded the bulky and fragile thermionic valves, making it possible to build small, lightweight radio transmitters and receivers.

Push buttons

98.1 FM

1 2 3 4 5 6 7 8 9 0 AM FM

− TUNE +

Radio Wave. The distance between successive peaks of a radio wave is its wavelength. The number of waves passing per second is its frequency, measured in Hertz (Hz). The height of the wave above its centre line is its amplitude.

Sound signals. Sound picked up by a microphone is turned into electrical signals which constantly vary. To transmit the sound, the pattern of the signals must be added to radio waves. This is called modulation. The radio wave that carries the sound signals is called a carrier wave.

AM radio wave. One way of transmitting sound is called Amplitude Modulation (AM), in which the amplitude of the radio wave is constantly varied by the signals from the microphone. However, AM signals are subject to electrical interference, which produces a crackling sound called static.

FM radio wave. In 1933, American engineer Edwin Armstrong (1890-1954) introduced Frequency Modulation (FM) radio, which is free from static. In FM radio signals, the frequency is constantly varied by signals from the microphone.

Inside a **transistor radio** complex electronics turn radio signals into sound. Integrated circuits containing thousands of transistors (see page 38) make it possible to produce very small radios. The radio has a rod aerial to pick up FM radio signals and a ferrite bar aerial for AM radio signals. Tuning is by push buttons which are more accurate than a moving pointer and tuning knob. A Liquid Crystal Display shows the frequency of the station to which the radio is tuned. The signals are a combination of sounds from right and left microphones. Stereo radios have extra circuits to separate right and left signals, and feed them to separate speakers.

The problem of interference between the early radio stations was solved by the British physicist Sir Oliver Lodge (1851-1940). By 'tuning' a transmitter and receiver to send and pick up only a particular radio frequency, many stations can operate at the same time.

A radio receiver picks up the weak electrical signals made by radio waves striking its aerial. These signals pass through tuned circuits which amplify them and pick out the signal to which the radio is tuned. The signal is next demodulated, removing the carrier wave but leaving the sound signal. This is amplified again before it reaches the loudspeaker, which turns the electrical signals into sound waves.

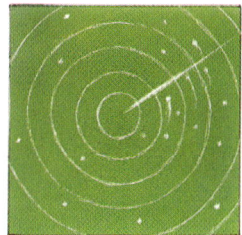

Microwave radio transmissions are used for radar and communication links, like outside broadcasts. Microwaves also will heat food in microwave ovens.

Infra-red radiation, another form of electromagnetic radiation, is given off by hot things. Special sensors detect it and produce heat pictures of objects.

Visible light is the only part of the electromagnetic spectrum we can see. The colours of the rainbow are lights of different frequencies.

Ultraviolet light is invisible. Excessive exposure to it can cause skin cancer. The ozone layer in the Earth's atmosphere stops much of it reaching us.

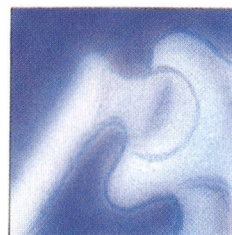

X-rays can pass through flesh but they are stopped by bones and metal. Like visible light, they can be used to take photographs.

Gamma rays are emitted by nuclear reactions and radioactive substances. They are extremely dangerous to all forms of life.

LISTENING IN
PERSONAL STEREO

The first personal stereo, the Sony Walkman, introduced in 1979, was the idea of Akio Morita (b. 1921), co-founder of the Japanese electronics company Sony. He wanted to produce a complete stereo cassette player not much larger than a cassette box, so both electronic and mechanical components had to be reduced in size. This idea of a 'personal' stereo proved a huge success.

Tape cassette

Ceramic tape guide reduces friction

The familiar tape cassette was introduced by the Dutch electronics firm Philips in 1963, together with a miniature tape recorder. Cassettes were simpler to use than anything else available and the sound quality was good. It was improved even more with the introduction of the Dolby system in 1966 (see opposite). Stereo signals are recorded on two different tracks of the tape, one for left-hand speakers, one for right-hand.

Magnetic tape

THE PERSONAL STEREO, a development of the cassette tape recorder, uses magnetic tape to play back sound. As the tape passes the play-back head, a magnetic pattern on the tape produces an electrical signal. This is fed through an amplifier to speakers, so you can hear the sound.

When you record something with a tape recorder, the microphone converts sound into an electric signal which is fed to electromagnets in the recording head. As the tape passes the recording head it is magnetised to create a magnetic pattern representing the original sound. When the tape passes the playback head, the process is reversed. Many modern tape recorders combine the recording and playback heads.

The earliest 'tape recorder' was invented by the Danish engineer Valdemar Poulsen in 1898. Called the 'Telegraphone', it was a telephone answering machine. It used steel wire, not tape. But there were no efficient amplifiers to boost the weak electric current it produced. In a modern cassette recorder the signals are amplified 100 billion times between head and speakers.

By the 1920s tape recorders using large reels of steel tape were in use, and in 1928 paper tapes with a magnetic coating were introduced. The familiar plastic tape appeared in 1935. It was developed by engineers trying to improve sticky tape for packaging! Plastic tape made small tape recorders possible, because it is much more magnetically sensitive than steel wire and tape. About 50 times more can be recorded on plastic tape, than on the steel tape.

The invention of silicon chips led to the development of miniature amplifiers and control systems. Without them there could be no personal stereos. A Dolby sound system chip is also incorporated, and another chip alters the power supply to the motor to regulate the tape's speed.

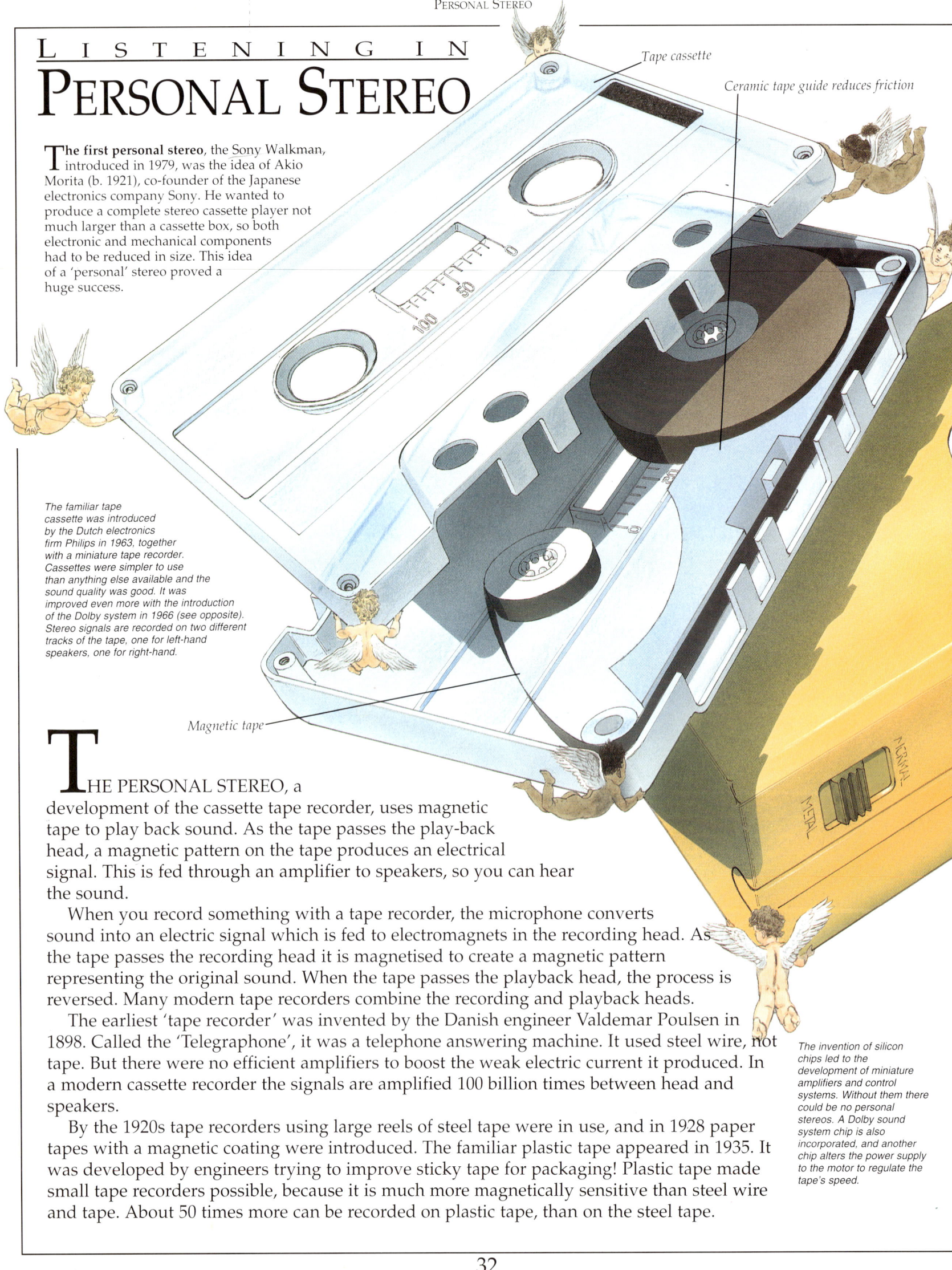

Personal stereos are designed to use little power, so they do not need bulky batteries. Inside is a circuit board containing the electronic components, volume control and sockets from the headphones. The tape in the cassette slots over spindles inside the personal stereo. A tiny electric motor turns the tape via a drive belt and gear wheels, making it move past the playback head. Most personal stereos are cassette players, but a few record as well.

Batteries

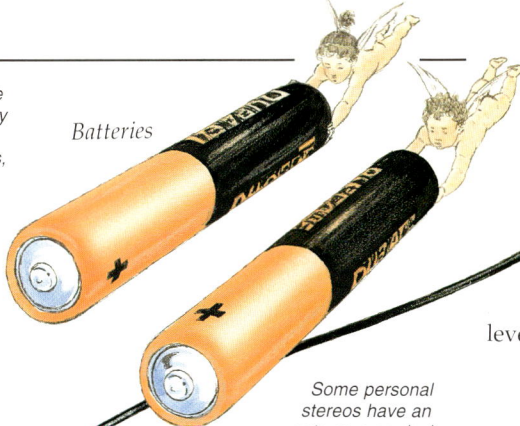

Some personal stereos have an auto-reverse device, so that both sides of the tape can be played without the cassette being taken out and turned over. You can also listen while running or jogging. However, one problem remains: sound leakage from the headphones.

One of the problems of tape recorders is the hiss, or background noise. In 1966 Ray Dolby introduced the Dolby noise reduction system to solve the problem. This increases the signal from the microphone when recording quiet passages, drowning out any hiss. When the tape is played, the Dolby system lowers the sound level for the quiet passages to the right level, reducing the hiss so you cannot hear it.

Most tape recorders and players are 'analogue', meaning that the magnetic pattern on the tape directly represents that of the sound recorded. In 1987, a different system, Digital Audio Tape (DAT), was introduced. The sound is converted electronically into a series of numbers, each representing the strength of the sound waves being recorded at a given moment, and these numbers are recorded on the tape in coded form. The DAT system is expensive, but gives much better sound quality.

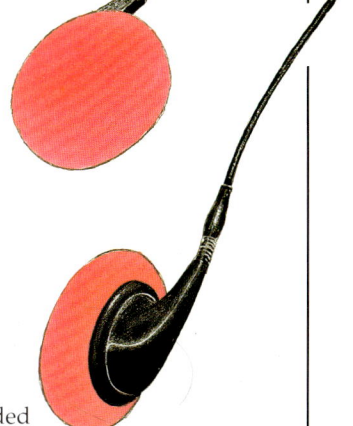

A personal stereo is too small to have built-in speakers, so headphones are used instead. Amplified electrical signals from the personal stereo are fed to electromagnets in the headphones which vibrate membranes to make a sound. In the Walkman plastic membranes are used, because they respond better than the usual metal.

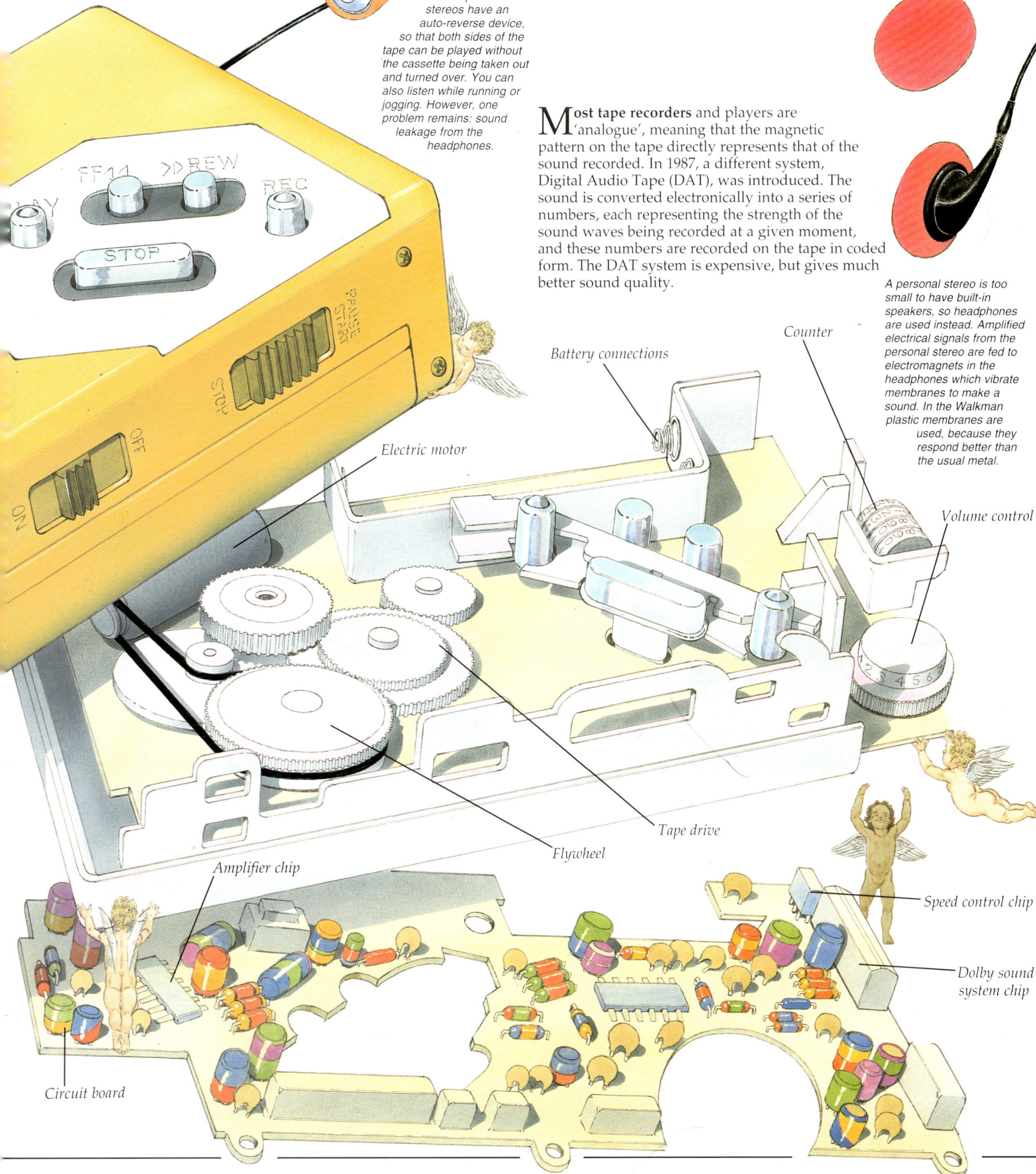

FF PLAY REW REC
STOP
PAUSE START STOP
OFF ON

Electric motor

Battery connections

Counter

Volume control

Tape drive

Flywheel

Amplifier chip

Speed control chip

Dolby sound system chip

Circuit board

Light enters the TV camera through the lens. Special mirrors split it into the three 'primary' colours: red, green and blue. Pictures are produced in each colour. Each colour picture is converted into electrical signals by a vidicon tube. Some TV cameras and most video cameras, use a

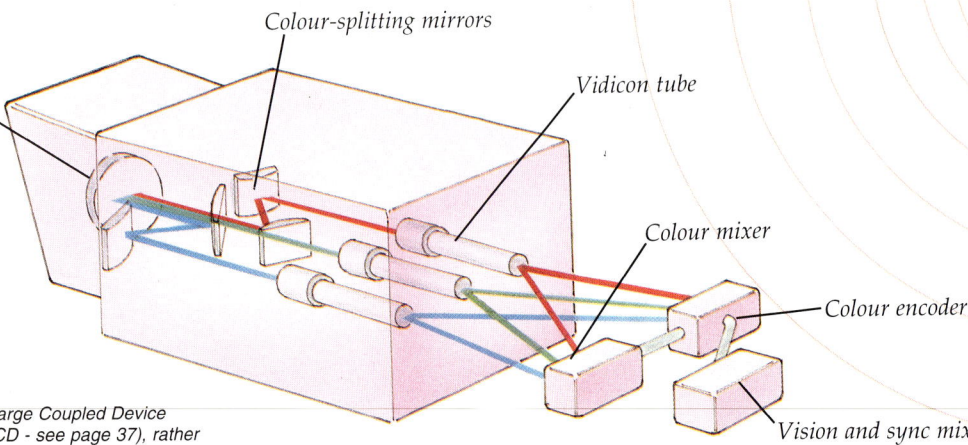

Colour-splitting mirrors

TV camera lens

Vidicon tube

Colour mixer

Colour encoder

Vision and sync mixer

Charge Coupled Device (CCD - see page 37), rather than mirrors and tubes, to produce the signals for each coloured picture.

Television does not actually transmit a continuously moving picture. It transmits 25 still pictures each second. Our eyes, however, see them as a moving picture.

The signals from the 3 camera tubes go to a colour encoder, which produces a signal for the colour of each part of the picture, and a colour mixer which produces a picture brightness signal.

A 'vision and sync mixer' adds a synchronizing signal to the signal from the camera, so the colour and brightness signals can be combined in the TV receiver.

The transmitter adds the amplified sound signal from the studio microphones and transmits the resulting TV signal. TV signals are usually broadcast on UHF radio waves. Different TV stations broadcast on different radio frequencies. The TV set selects which one, just like a radio.

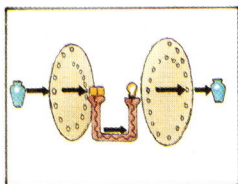

Cathode-ray oscilloscopes developed by the German scientist Ferdinand Braun (1850-1918) in 1897 were the ancestors of modern TV sets.

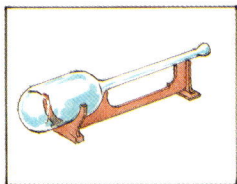

The Nipkow Disc, invented by the German engineer Paul Nipkow (1860-1940) in 1884, was used in television cameras and receivers until electronic cameras and TVs were invented in the 1930s.

The Scottish television pioneer John Logie Baird (1888-1946) made the first broadcasts in 1929 and did much to publicise television, although he did not invent it.

Baird's 1929 'Televisor' TVs produced fuzzy pictures which flickered badly. They were broadcast on medium wave radio signals unable to carry enough information for better pictures.

In 1936 the British Broadcasting Corporation (BBC) started the world's first high-definition TV service, soon replacing Baird's system with electronic TV cameras.

The Coronation of Britain's Queen Elizabeth II in 1953 was the first live, international TV broadcast of a major event.

Phosphor dots

Shadow mask

The back of a colour TV screen is coated with rows of red, green and blue phosphor dots. These glow when hit by one of the TV's three electron beams: one for each colour signal. A shadow mask behind the screen ensures the right beam hits the right dot. The TV actually produces separate red, green and blue pictures, but the eye blends them together.

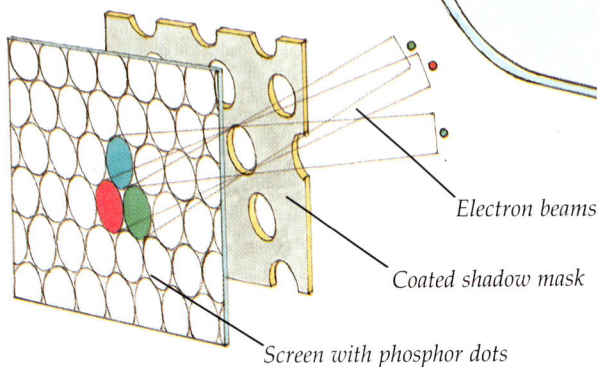

Electron beams

Coated shadow mask

Screen with phosphor dots

Aerial

Aerials like this pick up broadcast TV signals from transmitters within range. 'Dishes' receive signals broadcast from satellites in space. A dish aerial of mesh is as effective as a solid one.

VIEWING AT HOME
TELEVISION

A TV SYSTEM NEEDS A TV CAMERA to convert the picture into electric signals, and a TV receiver to convert the signals back into pictures. Television was first demonstrated in 1926 by the Scottish inventor John Logie Baird. His system of moving lenses and glowing bulbs was superseded in the 1930s by electronic systems. These used electron beams to scan and reproduce pictures and were the ancestors of today's TV camera and receivers. The first televisions transmitted moving pictures in the same way that radio (pages 30-31) transmits sound. Now, television pictures can also be transmitted through cables.

The first television service was started by the British Broadcasting Corporation in 1936. In the USA television broadcasts began in 1939. These early systems produced black and white pictures. Colour TV was developed in the USA in the 1950s, but colour televisions were not sold in large numbers until 1964, when they became cheaper thanks to improved designs and manufacturing. Europe's first colour TV broadcasts began in the UK in 1967.

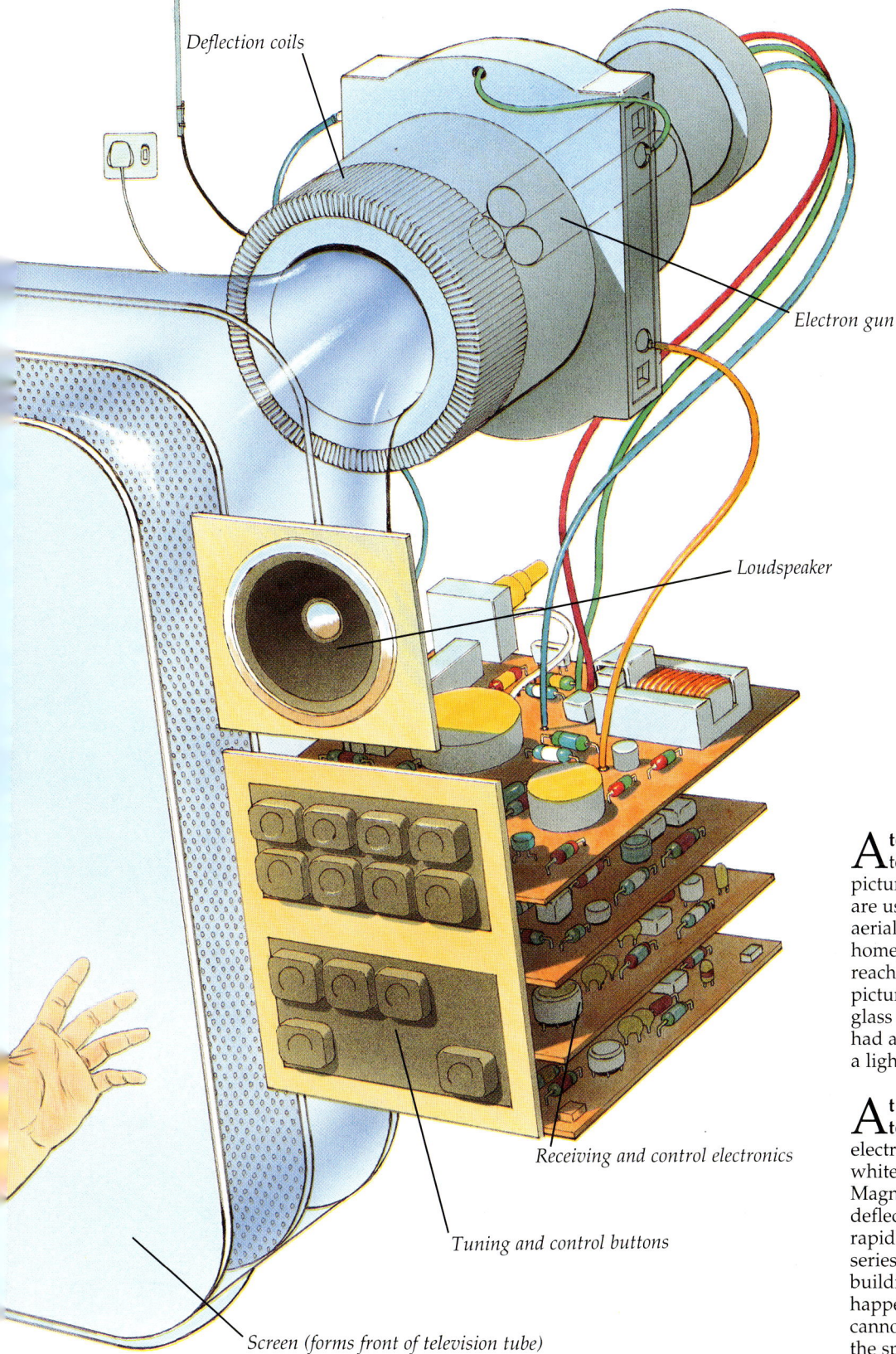

Deflection coils

Electron gun

Loudspeaker

Solar cell

Receiving and control electronics

Tuning and control buttons

Screen (forms front of television tube)

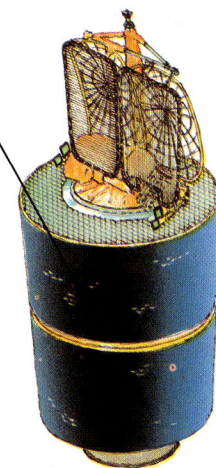

A television receiver turns television signals back into pictures and sound. The signals are usually picked up by an aerial on the roof of your home, by a satellite dish, or reach the home by cable. The pictures are reproduced by the glass television tube, which has had all the air sucked out (like a light bulb).

At the back of the television tube are three electron guns (a black and white TV has only one). Magnetic fields produced by deflector coils make the beams rapidly 'scan' the screen in a series of horizontal lines, building up the picture. All this happens so quickly, the eye cannot detect the movement of the spots of light. Modern TVs have 625 scanning lines.

In 1962 the words 'Live via satellite' first appeared on TV screens, when Telstar-1, the first communications satellite, came into service. Now satellites provide a global TV network, transmitting signals which can be picked up by a simple 'dish' on the side of a house.

VIEWING AT HOME

THE HOME VIDEO

THE HOME VIDEO recorder/player has radically changed the way we use our televisions. Favourite programmes can be recorded for viewing later, the newest films can be hired at video shops for home-viewing, and many other shops sell popular and specialist videos. Home cine films are now obsolete. Instead, camcorders, a combination of camera and video recorder, record scenes on to video tape cassettes which can be played back on the home video and shown on the television.

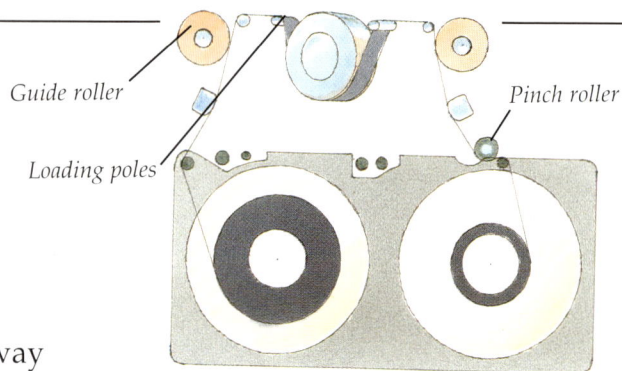

Guide roller

Pinch roller

Loading poles

The first successful video cassette system was the Sony U-Matic introduced in 1971. It was also the first to use this layout, but it was too big and expensive for home use.

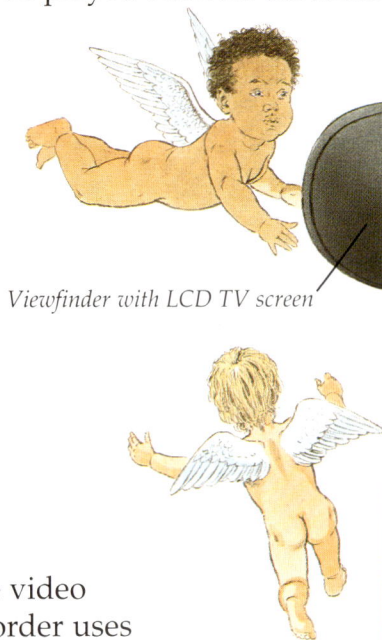

Tape cassette

Viewfinder with LCD TV screen

Video tape

The video recorder uses the magnetic tape technology of the audio tape recorder (see page 32) to record the signals from a television camera, and play them back later. Experimental video recorders were built in the early 1950s. However, because recording television pictures means storing much more information than recording sound signals, the early machines used vast amounts of tape – one and a half miles to record four minutes of video! The American company Ampex made the breakthrough, developing a method of recording video signals across the tape instead of parallel to it, so using less tape. A much modified version is used in today's video recorders and cameras. Ampex demonstrated their first video recorders in 1956, but the machines were large and expensive, and were used only by television companies. The first home video recorder, the Philips N1500, appeared in 1972. The Japanese electronics company Sony introduced the Betamax system in 1975, followed by JVC's rival VHS (Video Home System) in 1977. VHS, with longer playing time, proved more popular. But it was the introduction of small cassettes by Sony and JVC in the 1980s that made lighter camcorders possible.

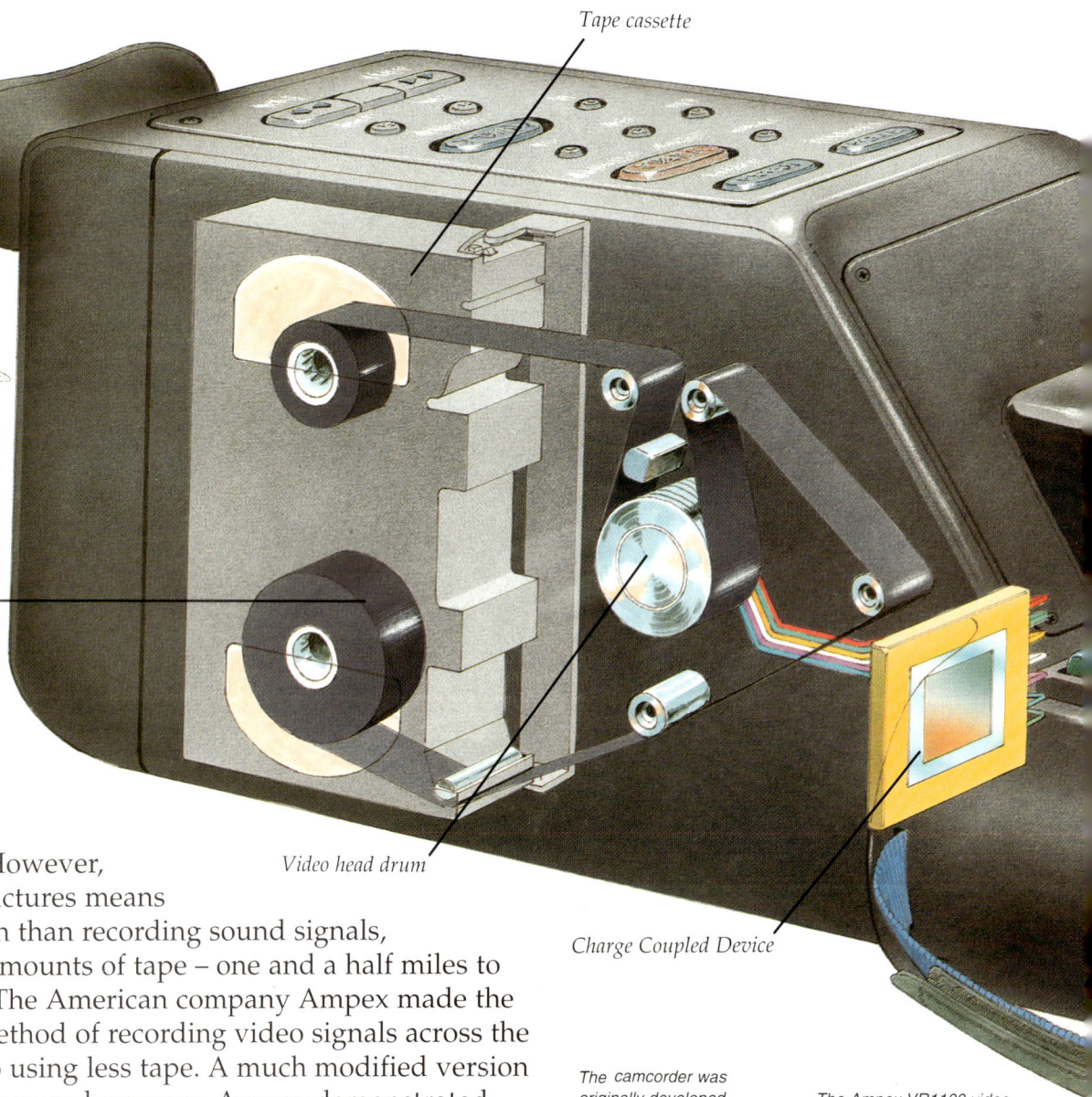

Video head drum

Charge Coupled Device

The camcorder was originally developed for television reporters. Before that, separate cameras and video recorders linked by cable were used. Home camcorders did not really become popular until after 1984, when Sony introduced the Video-8 camcorder. This used small cassettes, making it much smaller and lighter than its predecessors.

The Ampex VR1100 video recorder of 1956 was the first successful video recorder. The secrets of its success were the recording of information in parallel strips across the tape, instead of along it as in sound recording, and the mounting of the recording heads on a rapidly-spinning drum. Before video recording, television programmes were usually sent out live.

Guide roller

Erase head

Loading poles

Rotating drum carrying recording and replay heads

Put a video cassette into the recorder and loading poles pull a loop of tape out of the cassette and around guide rollers and the drum containing the recording and playback heads.

When a new recording is made the erase head wipes existing recordings off the tape. The sound and control heads record or replay the sound and picture control signals.

Loading poles pull tape out of cassette when loaded and bring it to the rollers and heads

Audio and control signal replay head

Recording and replay heads

Picture **information** is recorded as diagonal lines across the video tape. A continuous sound track runs along one edge of the tape and a control track along the other.

Pinch roller presses tape against capstan

Rotating capstan to move tape through recorder

A picture contains more information than a sound signal so, when recording a picture, the tape must pass the recording heads much faster than in an audio tape recorder. This is achieved with a scanning system. The recording heads are mounted on a rapidly-spinning drum set at an angle to the slowly-moving tape. Each time the drum rotates, a television picture is recorded or replayed. Every second, 25 pictures are transmitted to the television screen, creating the illusion of movement.

Microphone

Zoom lens

The pictures recorded by the Ampex VR1100 video recorder were poor by today's standards, but by 1956 standards they were high-quality.

Light passing through the camera lens is focused onto a Charge Coupled Device. The CCD is composed of thousands of tiny light-sensitive cells. In a video camera, these are arranged in groups of three, each sensitive to a different colour, to record colour information. The CCD converts the picture into an electrical pattern, which is coded and recorded onto the video tape.

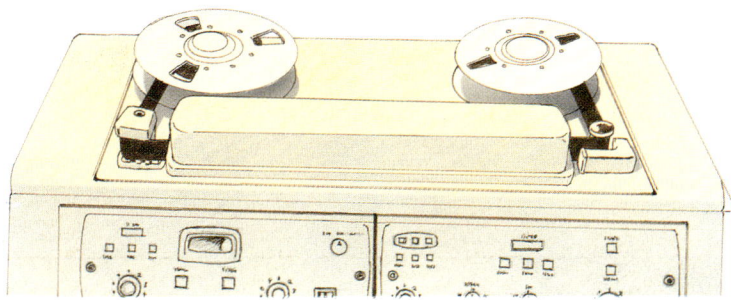

SILICON CHIPS AT WORK
THE POCKET CALCULATOR

5.1875

A SIMPLE POCKET CALCULATOR has a keyboard to input numbers and instruct the calculator to add, multiply, divide, subtract and display the results of the calculations on a Liquid Crystal Display (LCD). Under the keyboard is a printed circuit board with sets of contacts for each key. Also on the circuit board are the microprocessor which does the calculations, the LCD and a solar cell which converts light into electrical energy to work the calculator. The microprocessor works like a small, limited computer. It has a program containing instructions on how to make calculations and a memory to store the program.

The microprocessor is a miniature electronic device called an 'integrated circuit' or 'silicon chip'. Each chip is a piece of silicon containing a complicated network of electronic circuits. The circuits may consist of millions of tiny electronic devices, such as transistors and diodes and their connections. Chips are built up, layer by layer (below and opposite), in a complex photographic etching process, which is why they can be so small.

Although silicon chips are relatively inexpensive, the equipment to make them costs millions of pounds. Cleanliness, pure materials and quality control are vital. One speck of dust or minute impurity can shut down a production line, ruining a batch of chips, numbering many thousands.

The processes by which a chip is built up are very complex and can take weeks. The drawings (right) show a greatly simplified version of how a single component of a chip, a transistor, is produced. The first successful integrated circuits were produced in 1959 by the American company Texas Instruments. By 1978 it was possible to compress the Central Processing Unit (CPU) of a computer into a tiny chip, and the first microprocessors appeared.

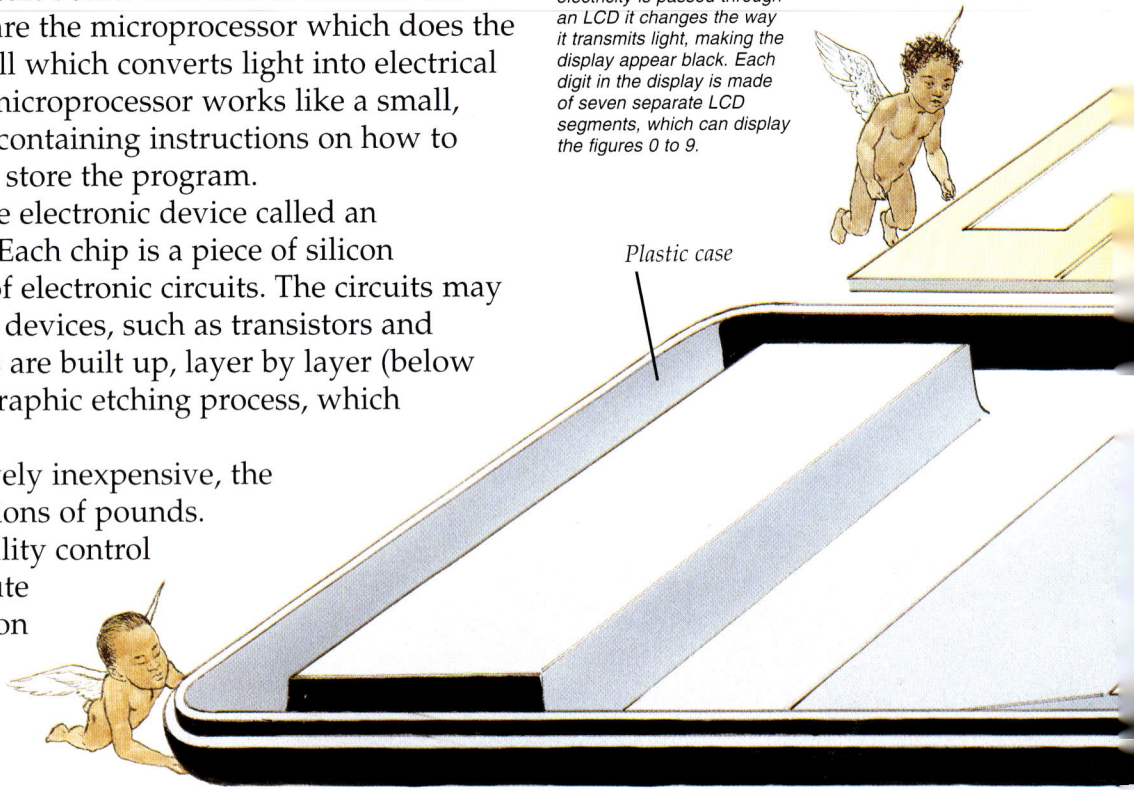

The numbers input to the calculator and the results of calculations are shown on a Liquid Crystal Display (LCD). LCDs are small and light and use little electricity, so are ideal for electronic gadgets such as watches and calculators. When electricity is passed through an LCD it changes the way it transmits light, making the display appear black. Each digit in the display is made of seven separate LCD segments, which can display the figures 0 to 9.

Plastic case

MAKING A CHIP

First make pure silicon dioxide, an electrical insulator and the main component of sand. To do this, silicon is melted. This starts a crystallization process. As a crystal forms, it is drawn from the molten silicon, producing a crystal about 100mm in diameter and up to a metre long.

The crystal of silicon is ground to make it completely smooth and round, then cut into wafers about 0.25mm thick. These are polished and cleaned.

Then a layer of silicon dioxide is formed on one side by heating the wafers in a furnace containing an oxidizing gas.

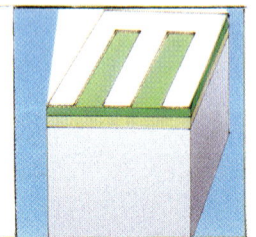

A 'photoresistant' layer, which hardens when exposed to ultraviolet (UV) light, is added. The circuit pattern mask is put on top and the wafer exposed to UV light.

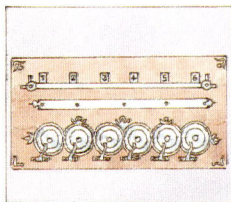

HISTORY OF COMPUTERS

The French mathematician Blaise Pascal (1623-1662) invented this calculator in 1642 to help his tax-collector father.

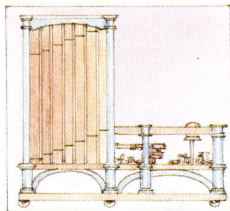

Charles Babbage (1791-1871) designed his Difference Engine in the 1820s to eliminate human error in calculating.

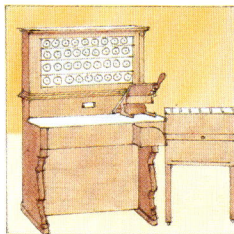

Herman Hollerith (1860-1929), an American engineer, developed a system for analysing census data using punched cards.

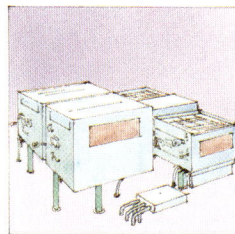

The Manchester University Differential Analyser of 1935 was an early mechanical computer used to design telecommunications networks.

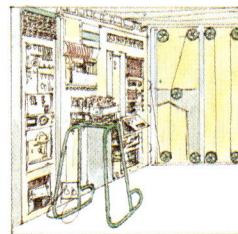

Colossus was a British electronic code-cracking machine built in 1943 to decipher German secret messages.

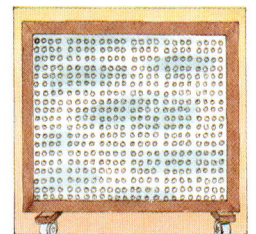

ENIAC (Electronic Numerical Integrator And Computer), the first modern electronic computer, was built in 1945 for the US Army.

The calculator contains a circuit which checks if the solar cell is providing enough power to run the calculator. If it is, the LCD comes on.

Microprocessor behind solar cell

Liquid Crystal Display

Solar cell

Rubber keypad

Push-button key contacts

Printed circuit board

A microprocessor silicon chip (above) about this size and costing £1,000 can be half as powerful as a 1976 Cray Supercomputer which cost £20,000,000.

Pressing a button (left) pushes the key contacts against a metal pad, closing the circuit and sending a signal to the microprocessor.

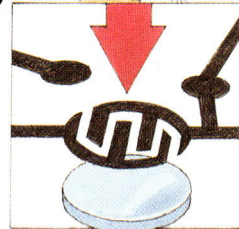

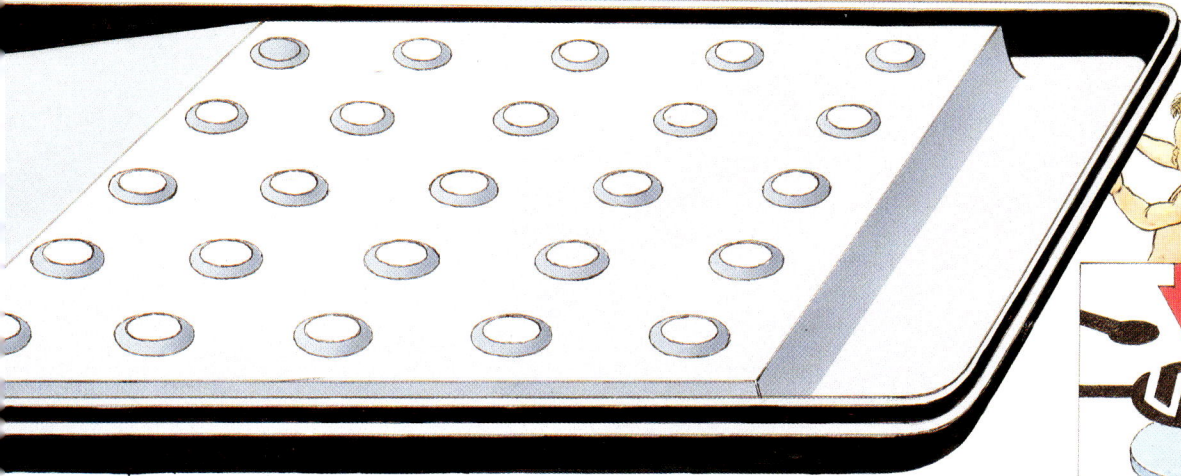

The mask is removed. The covered areas have stayed soft, and are now washed away with solvents to expose the silicon dioxide layer underneath.

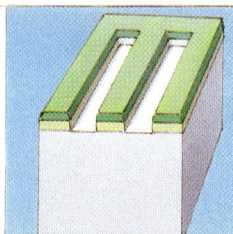

The silicon dioxide layer that this process exposes is then dissolved away with acid to expose the silicon beneath it.

The photoresistant layer is then removed. The areas of silicon revealed by the acid process are 'doped' to change their electrical properties.

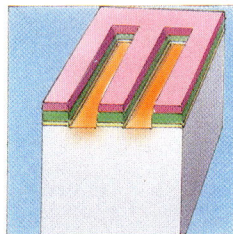

The processes are then repeated, with different-shaped masks, to build up all the different layers and components in the chip.

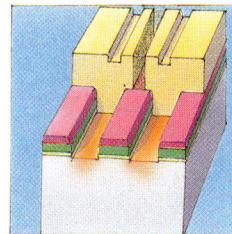

A layer of aluminium is then deposited on the chip. A final series of masking and etching processes turn the layer into electrical connections.

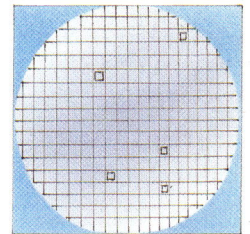

Before the wafers are cut up into hundreds of silicon chips, each chip is tested. The failure rate may be as high as 70%.

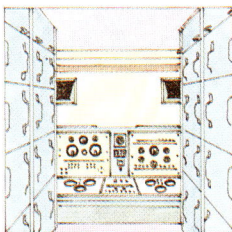

The Lyons Electronic Office (LEO) of 1951 was a pioneering British computer. It did the accounts of the catering company, J. Lyons.

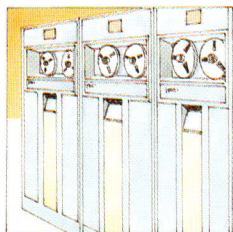

The CDC 6600 of 1963 was the largest and the most powerful computer of the big 'mainframe' computers built at this time.

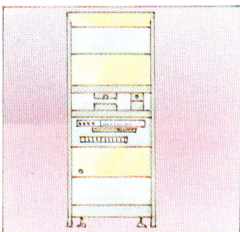

The PDP-8 of 1963 was the first minicomputer. Using transistors, it made limited computing power available very cheaply.

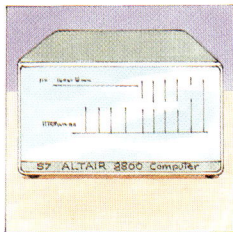

In 1975 the development of the microprocessor made smaller computers possible. The Altair of 1975 was the first home computer.

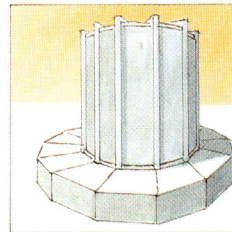

The CRAY 1/A was the first of the new fast, powerful supercomputers, used for specialist research, such as modelling weather patterns.

The Apple II of 1976 was the first really popular PC. It was deliberately designed to be 'user-friendly' – easy to use by non-experts.

SILICON CHIPS AT WORK
THE PERSONAL COMPUTER

Introduced in the late 1970s, personal computers (PCs) are now essential office tools. They are used for word processing (replacing typewriters), doing accounts and producing simple illustrations. At home, video game consoles are another, specialised form of PC.

At the heart of a PC are a number of 'integrated circuits' or 'silicon chips'. These store and process the information needed to start up and operate the computer. The most important of these circuits is the Central Processing Unit (CPU), but a PC also has other electrical devices. A power supply converts mains electricity into the correct current and voltage to operate the PC. A cooling fan stops it from overheating, because all the electronics produce heat. Disc drives transfer information to and from rotating magnetic discs which are used to store both the programs which the computer runs and the instructions for the computer to run them. The discs are also used to transfer information and programs between PCs.

A keyboard enables the user to control the PC and to input information. Wires plugged into output ports transmit information to a TV monitor or visual display unit (VDU) or a printer.

The silicon chips inside a PC have mysterious names: RAM, ROM and CPU. What they do is described opposite.

Hard disc drive

Most PCs have a mouse, a hand-held device attached to the PC by a wire 'tail'.

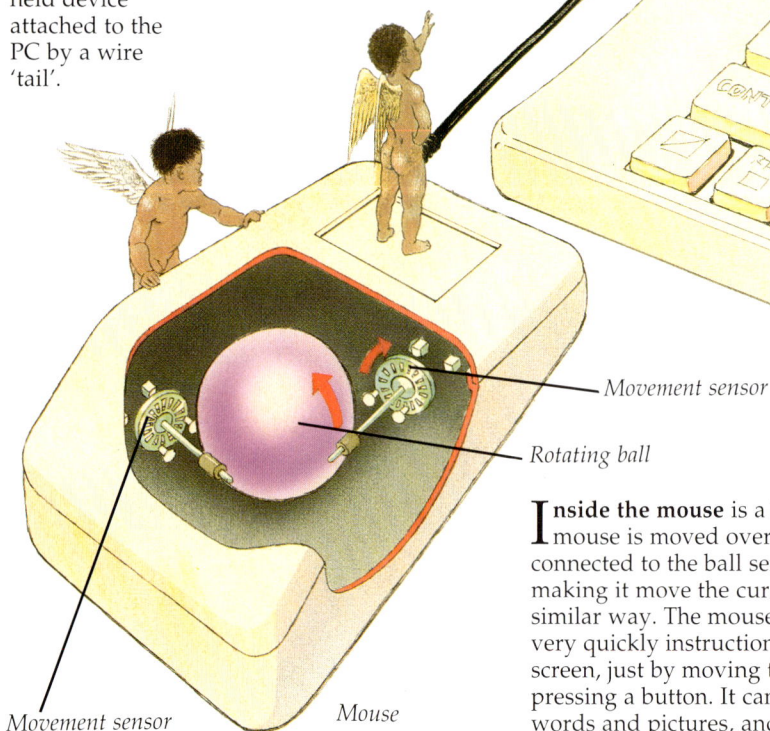

Movement sensor

Rotating ball

Movement sensor

Mouse

Keyboard

Inside the mouse is a ball which turns as the mouse is moved over a flat surface. Sensors connected to the ball send signals to the PC, making it move the cursor on the screen in a similar way. The mouse can be used to select very quickly instructions displayed on the screen, just by moving the cursor to them and pressing a button. It can also be used to move words and pictures, and to draw lines.

A PC's keyboard is like that of a typewriter. However, instead of mechanical linkages, the keys make electrical contacts which send signals to the PC. Besides the familiar letters and numbers, function keys instruct the PC to carry out programmed tasks, such as starting up the PC, moving the cursor around the screen and storing programs.

The ROM (Read-Only Memory) chip permanently stores instructions for starting the PC and for the CPU that controls it.

The CPU (Central Processing Unit) chip (or microprocessor) runs the computer program, receiving data from the keyboard and outputting results.

The RAM (Random Access Memory) chips temporarily store the program being used. Switching off the PC wipes them clean.

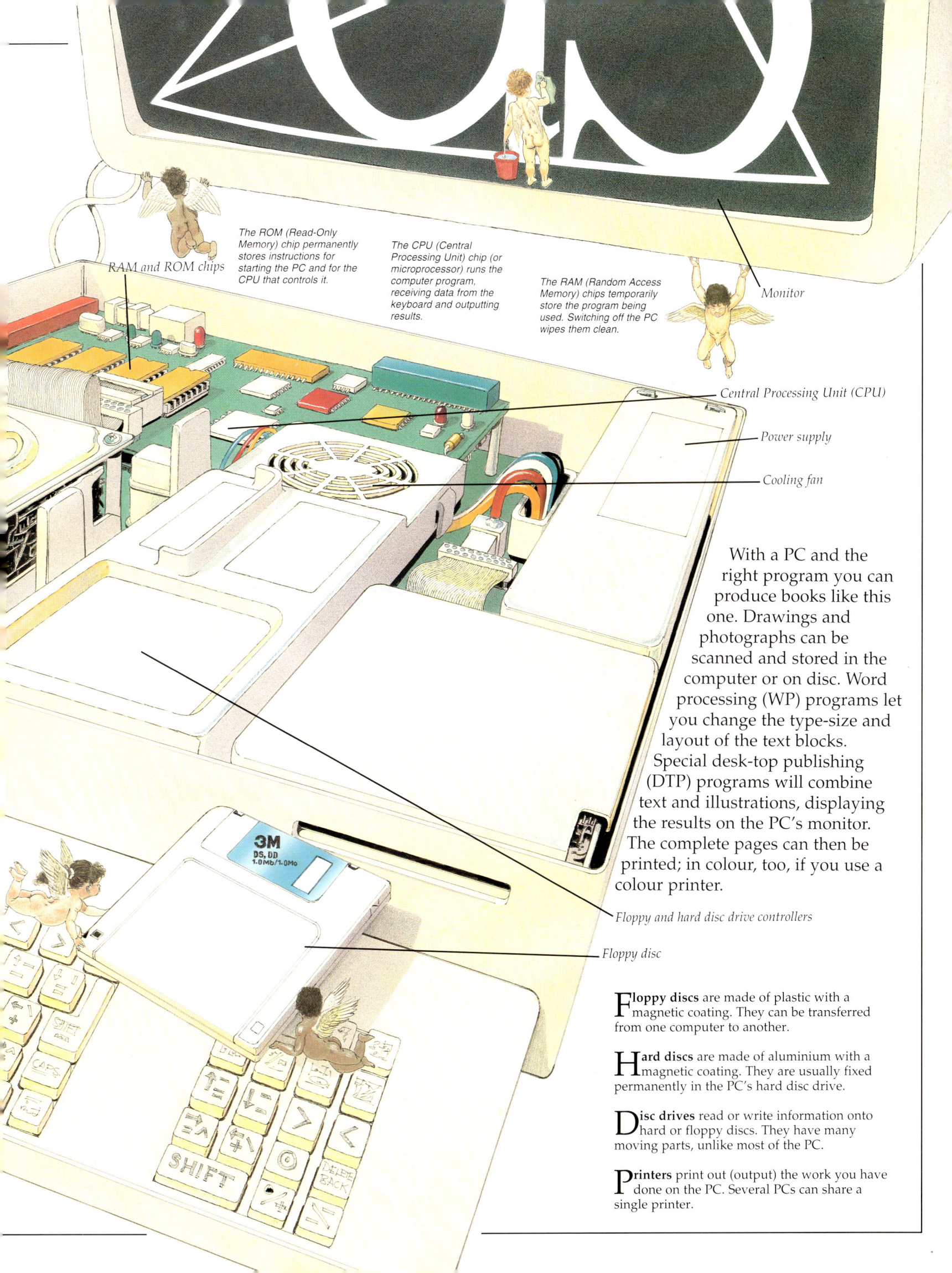

RAM and ROM chips

Monitor

Central Processing Unit (CPU)

Power supply

Cooling fan

With a PC and the right program you can produce books like this one. Drawings and photographs can be scanned and stored in the computer or on disc. Word processing (WP) programs let you change the type-size and layout of the text blocks. Special desk-top publishing (DTP) programs will combine text and illustrations, displaying the results on the PC's monitor. The complete pages can then be printed; in colour, too, if you use a colour printer.

Floppy and hard disc drive controllers

Floppy disc

3M
DS, DD
1.0 Mb/1.0 Mo

Floppy discs are made of plastic with a magnetic coating. They can be transferred from one computer to another.

Hard discs are made of aluminium with a magnetic coating. They are usually fixed permanently in the PC's hard disc drive.

Disc drives read or write information onto hard or floppy discs. They have many moving parts, unlike most of the PC.

Printers print out (output) the work you have done on the PC. Several PCs can share a single printer.

SHIFT
CAPS
DELETE BACK

READING WITH A DIFFERENCE
MAGNETIC CARDS AND BAR-CODES

Ticket ejected here

Ticket slot

Gates open
if ticket valid

Magnetic strip

The ticket is put
into a slot in the
gate and 'read'. If it is
valid, the gate opens
when you walk past
an infra-red beam.
The machine then
returns, retains or
cancels your ticket.

Code reading
and ticket
cancelling
mechanism

DURING THE 1970s the price of computers fell,
due to the development of microprocessors (page 39).
These can process complex information and codes so
quickly that they led to a revolution in the way we
pay for goods and services. Instead of cash or cheques,
we can now use plastic cards with magnetic strips
which contain information about us. Some cards
(smart cards) contain microprocessors to store even
more information.

A card reader at the till reads the card just as a tape
recorder reads a tape. The same technology is used in
automatic ticket gates at railway stations, where a
machine reads the tickets instead of a ticket inspector.

Communications are vital to the processing of the
information on these plastic cards. Most systems rely
on the card reader communicating electronically with
a central computer. Unfortunately, it is possible to fake
the cards and their magnetic strips, so this new
technology creates new opportunities for crime as well
as making shopping easier.

AUTHORISED SIGNATURE

VISA

Card slot

The
magnetic
strip on a
cashpoint card
has separate
tracks (like audio
tape) for your
name, account
number and
banking information.
A hologram makes
the card harder to fake.

Hologram makes
forgery harder

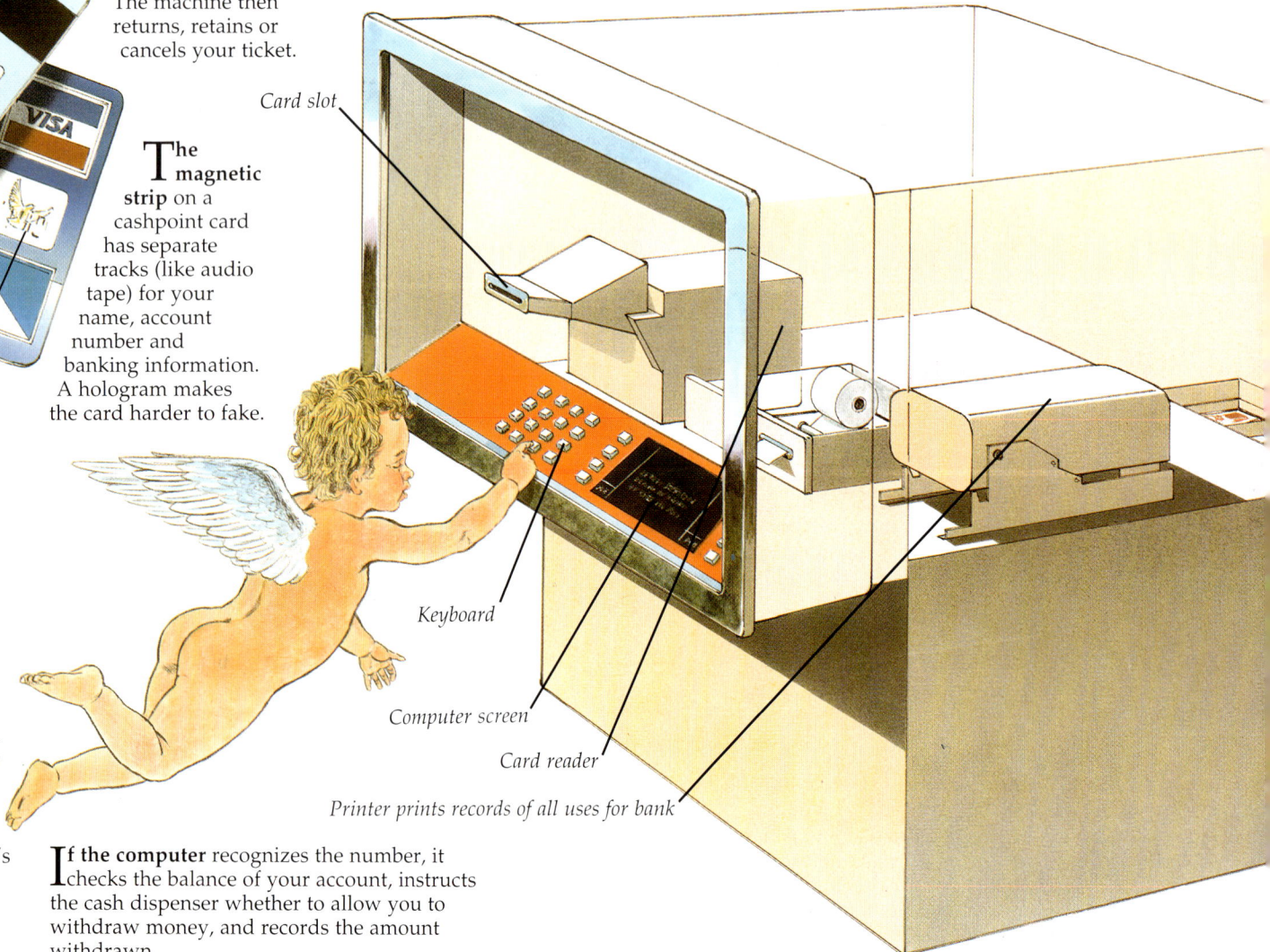

Keyboard

Computer screen

Card reader

Printer prints records of all uses for bank

Cash dispensers
'read' your bank
card. Typing in your
PIN (Personal
Identification
Number), sends a
message to the bank's
central computer
many miles away,
which checks the
number.

If the computer recognizes the number, it
checks the balance of your account, instructs
the cash dispenser whether to allow you to
withdraw money, and records the amount
withdrawn.

In 1970 a different way of reading information about goods was introduced: the bar-code. This is a label printed with a series of black stripes and white spaces. There is one on the jacket of this book. The thickness of the stripes and spaces corresponds to a code which can be understood by a computer, giving it information about a particular item. For example, many libraries now use bar codes. When you borrow a book, the librarian scans the bar-codes on your library ticket and the book with a light pen, which shines an infra-red laser beam onto the bar-code. Only the white spaces reflect the light. When the light pen is moved over the bar-code, the reflected rays are picked up by a sensor, which sends a series of electrical pulses to the scanner for decoding. The information goes to a central computer which records that you have borrowed the book and when it is due back. The scanner usually has a date stamp, set by the computer, which prints the book's return date on its library label.

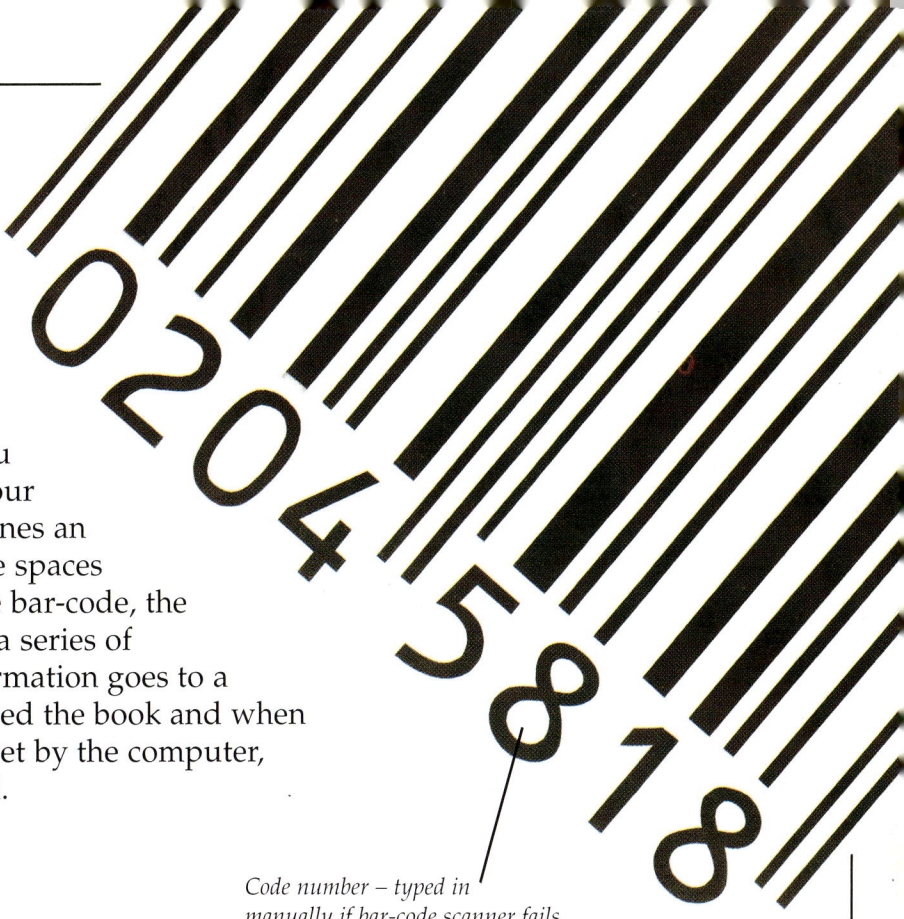

Code number – typed in manually if bar-code scanner fails

T**he Article Numbering Organisation** standardises bar-code numbers. The codes identify product, manufacturer and country. The numbers represented by the code are printed below it.

Bar-code scanner under here

M**ost supermarkets** and many smaller shops now have laser checkouts. These have many advantages. Queues move more quickly and it's more difficult for the assistant to make mistakes. The equipment produces detailed lists of everything you have bought. You can also pay with a debit card because the checkout's equipment is linked to magnetic card readers. The checkouts are linked to the shop's central computer system, which records how fast or slowly each item is selling. This makes reordering easy and efficient. Laser checkouts work in a similar way to hand-held bar-code scanners. However, underneath the slot in the checkout a spinning disc deflects the infra-red laser beam, making it scan across the slot so the bar-codes can be read at any angle. If the scanner cannot read the code the assistant uses the keyboard to tap it in directly.

Cash drawers

Money dispenser

Keyboard and card reader

Display unit shows goods and prices

READING WITH A DIFFERENCE

LASERS

THE WORD LASER stands for Light Application by the Stimulated Emission of Radiation. Lasers produce narrow beams of either intense light or infra-red rays. When the laser was invented in 1960, it was little more than a useless scientific curiosity. Now they are common. Every home with a compact disc (CD) player has a laser and every supermarket checkout with bar-code readers has them. They are also used with optical fibre cables to produce more efficient computer data and phone lines.

The compact disc, introduced in 1980, has gradually replaced the vinyl records used in home stereo systems. Instead of a sharp stylus moving along a record groove, CDs are 'read' by a beam of laser light - nothing touches the disc, so it cannot wear out. (Video discs, working on a similar principle, are used instead of video tape to store films.) Because they can store large amounts of information, CDs are also used in personal computers, as CD-ROM storing, for example, the text and pictures of an encyclopaedia. There are also 'Multimedia' CDs containing text, still pictures, sound and video.

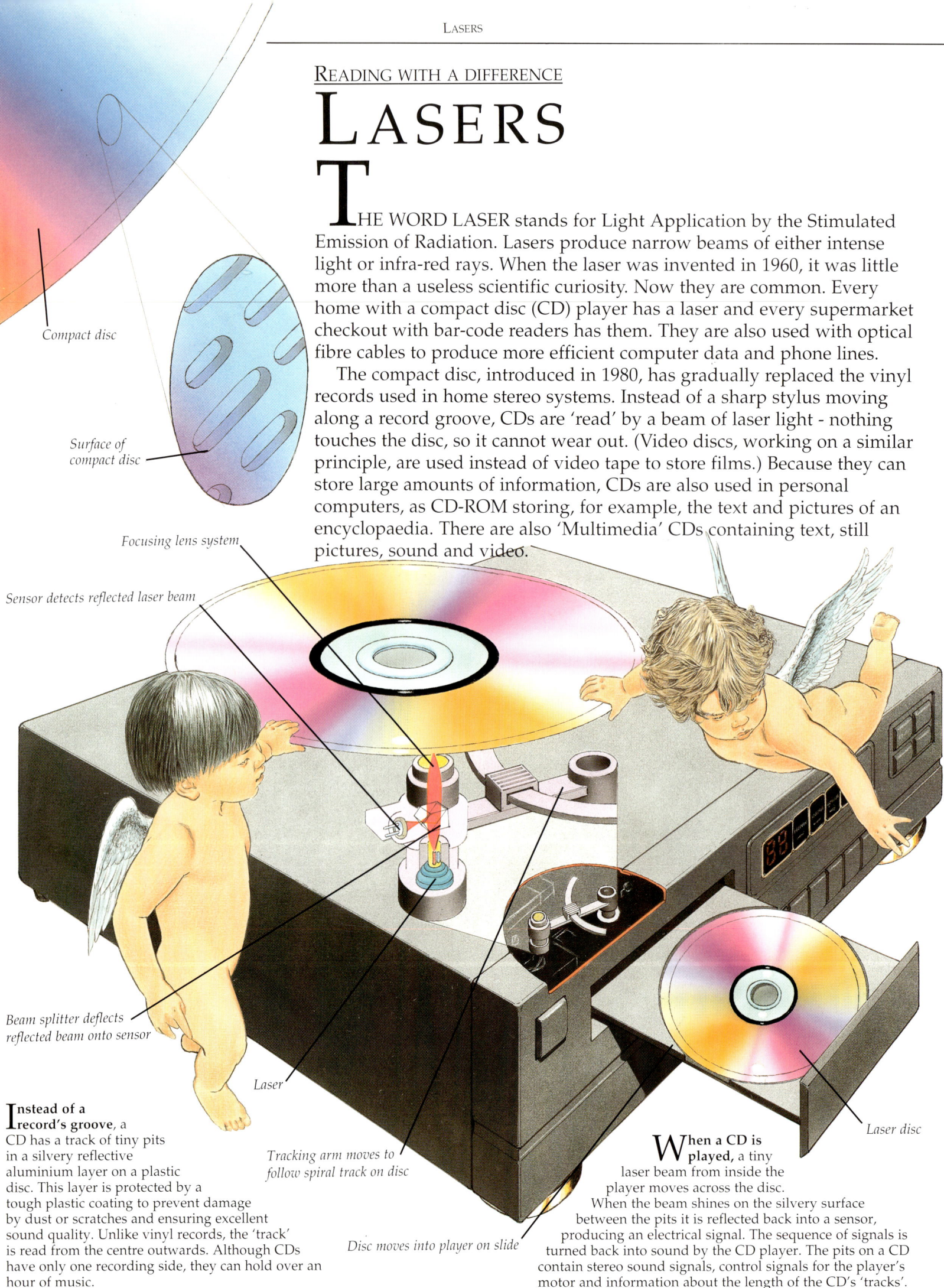

Compact disc

Surface of compact disc

Focusing lens system

Sensor detects reflected laser beam

Beam splitter deflects reflected beam onto sensor

Laser

Tracking arm moves to follow spiral track on disc

Disc moves into player on slide

Laser disc

Instead of a record's groove, a CD has a track of tiny pits in a silvery reflective aluminium layer on a plastic disc. This layer is protected by a tough plastic coating to prevent damage by dust or scratches and ensuring excellent sound quality. Unlike vinyl records, the 'track' is read from the centre outwards. Although CDs have only one recording side, they can hold over an hour of music.

When a CD is played, a tiny laser beam from inside the player moves across the disc. When the beam shines on the silvery surface between the pits it is reflected back into a sensor, producing an electrical signal. The sequence of signals is turned back into sound by the CD player. The pits on a CD contain stereo sound signals, control signals for the player's motor and information about the length of the CD's 'tracks'.

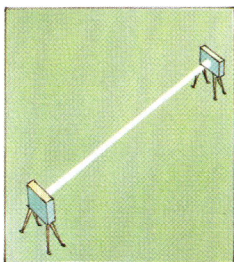

Electronically timing the movement of a laser pulse between two points gives the distance between them. The laser tape measure works on this principle.

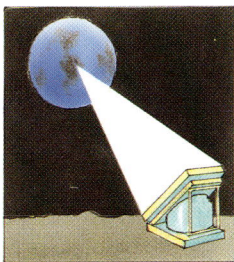

A narrow laser beam is bright enough to reach the moon. Measuring the time taken for the beam to be reflected back gives you the moon's distance.

Sea depths are measured with green lasers which can pass through several hundred metres of water. The principle is the same as the laser tape measure

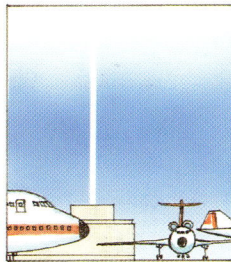

Laser beams reflected by the water droplets in clouds are used at airports to measure cloud height. This is especially useful to pilots at night.

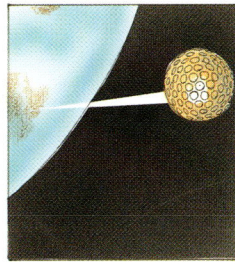

The Lageos satellite is studded with reflectors, so laser measurements of its distance can be taken to trace tiny movements of the earth's surface.

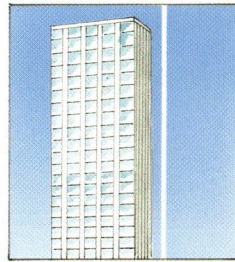

Tiny changes in distance are measured by an Interferometer. This uses laser beams and has an accuracy of half a millionth of a metre.

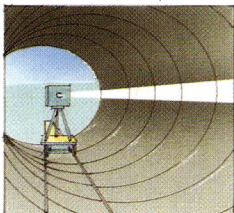

The straight, thin beam of light from a laser can be used as a guide for aligning pipes and tunnels. The Channel Tunnel was aligned using lasers.

Specially equipped vans bounce lasers off a road surface to find out about its condition. This is a quick, efficient way of surveying roads.

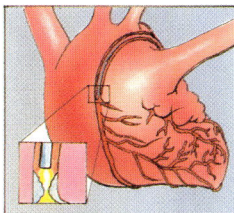

A laser beam transmitted through an optical fibre cable can remove fat from blood vessels in treating heart disease.

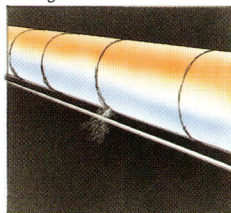

Gas leaking from a pipe can be detected by monitoring changes in the brightness of a laser beam shining along the outside of the pipe.

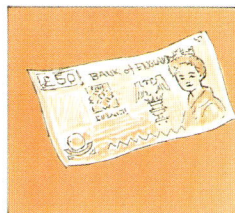

High-value bank notes contain patterned metal strips cut by laser. This makes them much harder to forge.

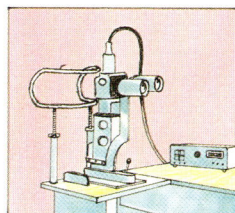

Tiny holes drilled in the eye with a laser can cure sight problems caused by increased pressure in the eyeball.

Using a laser to project a picture of an aircraft's instruments on to the windscreen means the pilots can see them without looking down.

Looking at a special pattern made by the beam of a laser eye-testing machine will show whether a patient is short- or long-sighted.

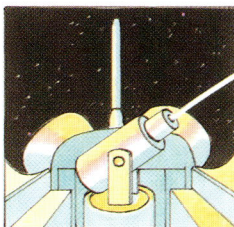

Space shuttle crews sent to repair satellites use lasers to measure the distance between the two spacecraft, to make recovering the satellite easier.

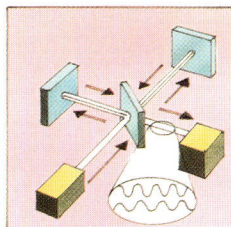

A laser beam can also be used for vertical alignment, replacing the traditional plumb-line. Electronic equipment measures the angle of the laser's line.

Fingerprint patterns can be scanned by lasers and the information stored on computer for police searches or to operate fingerprint-activated locks.

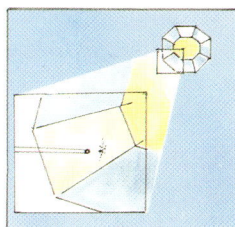

Laser beams produce enough heat to make holes in diamonds – the hardest known substance. They can remove flaws, or etch on security identifications.

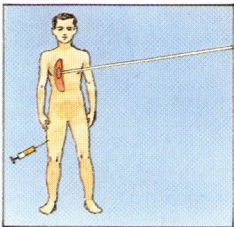

Lasers can treat some cancer tumours. Special chemicals absorbed by cancer cells are converted by laser light into poison which destroys the tumour.

Breaking the pattern of laser beams in a laser 'harp' sends signals to an electronic music synthesiser, so producing sound.

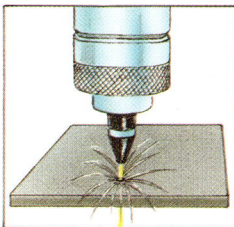

Laser beams are intense enough to 'drill' holes in metal. They heat a small patch so it first melts and then boils away.

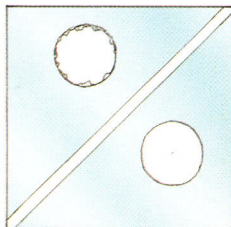

Lasers are fired in short powerful bursts to make holes. They are especially good for cutting soft or springy materials, like plastic, cloth and paper.

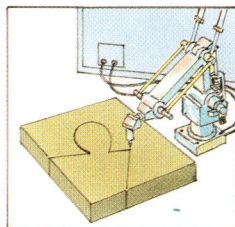

An industrial robot fitted with a laser can be programmed to move it over the surface to be cut.

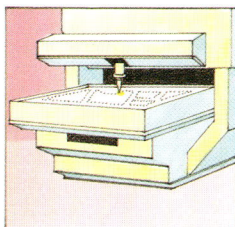

Cutting metal with a laser: the laser moves from left to right as the sheet slides in and out of the computer-controlled machines.

Laser light can be used to take special photographs called holograms, three-dimensional pictures, which appear to have depth just like the real object.

Holograms can be printed onto silvery plastic, but these lack the sharpness of the original. They are used for books, jewellery, packaging and bank cards.

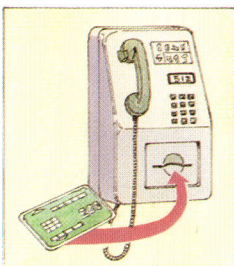

Phone cards have a hologram strip. Each time the card is used, the phone destroys part of the hologram until the card is used up.

Stresses in machinery will show up as wavy lines in double-exposure holograms taken of the parts when they are moving and stationary.

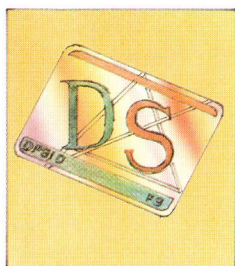

Holograms are printed on many types of credit and bank cards. Because holograms are difficult to make, forging these cards is extremely hard.

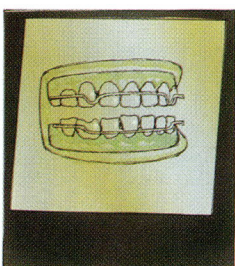

Holograms look so like real objects that they are used to record details of things as different as the insides of nuclear reactors and works of art.

GLOSSARY

NOTE: Some of the words in this Glossary have more than one meaning. The meaning given here relates to the topics described in this book. Words printed in italics have entries in this Glossary.

AC electricity (Alternating Current electricity) Electric current that reverses (alternates) its direction regularly. AC electricity is produced by electric generators called *alternators*.

Alternator Electric generator which produces alternating and not direct current. See *AC electricity* and *DC electricity*.

AM (Amplitude Modulation) Means of transmitting sound using radio signals. The *amplitude* of the *radio wave* is varied to match the electric signal from the microphone.

Amplitude The size of a wave. Waves are the way in which some kinds of energy, such as sound and radio signals, travel.

Battery Container in which an electric current is produced by mixing different materials and chemicals.

Carrier wave *Radio wave* modified to 'carry' sound signals from a microphone.

Cathode ray The stream of invisible particles called electrons that flows from the part of an electrical device, such as a *battery*, called a cathode.

CCD (Charge Coupled Device) A special form of *integrated circuit* which converts pictures into electrical signals.

CD-ROM (Compact Disc-Read Only Memory) Way of storing information on compact discs which can be read by computers. Text, pictures, motion pictures and sound can all be stored on the same disc.

Cellular telephone Portable telephone linked by radio to a network of local radio stations, or cells, and from them to the main telephone network.

Circuit board Piece of plastic carrying components which make up the electronic circuits in equipment such as radios, videos and computers.

DAT (Digital Audio Tape) Improved method of recording sound signals on magnetic tape, using *digital* instead of analogue signals.

DC electricity (Direct Current electricity) Electric current that flows in only one direction. It is produced by DC generators and batteries.

Demodulate To separate *sound* and *carrier wave* signals from the radio broadcast signal. This is done in a radio *receiver*.

Digital Information, such as computer programs, sound signals or pictures, recorded as a sequence of numbers.

Diode Electronic device through which electricity can only flow in one direction. *Thermionic valves* were early diodes. Modern diodes are made from *semiconductors*.

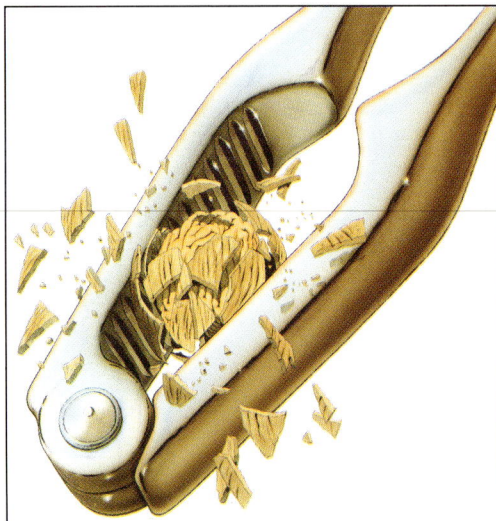

Disc drive The part of a computer that 'reads' or 'writes' information from or onto *floppy discs* or *hard discs*.

Doping Changing the electrical properties of materials by adding impurities, such as boron, antimony, arsenic or indium, to produce *semiconductors*. See also *transistors* and *diodes*.

Electric current Flow of electrons along an electrical conductor, transferring electrical energy.

Electricity Form of *energy* that can be easily produced, transmitted and converted to other forms of energy, such as light, heat, sound or movement.

Electromagnet Magnet that uses electricity to produce magnetism. These magnets can be turned on and off with the flow of the electric current.

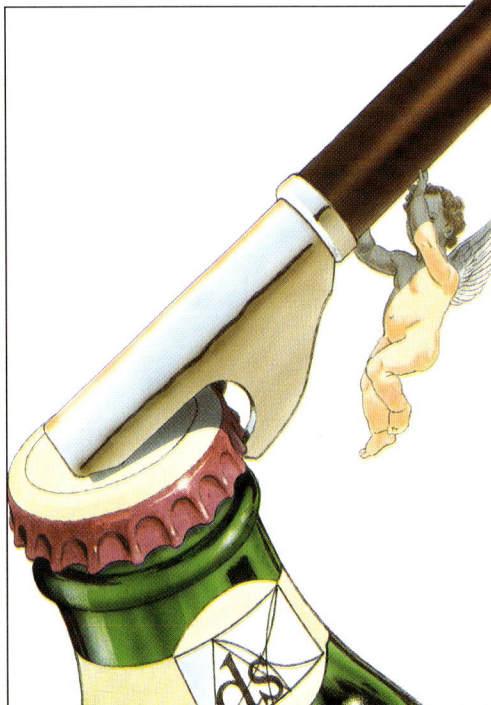

Electromagnetic radiation Form of electric and magnetic *energy* that can travel through space. Radio waves, visible light and X-rays are all types of electromagnetic radiation.

Electron beam The stream of electrons (one of the three types of particles from which atoms are made) produced by an *electron gun*.

Electron gun The part of a television set which fires a beam of invisible particles, called electrons, at the screen to produce the picture.

Electronic Any device that works by the flow of *electricity* through a gas, vacuum or *semiconductor*, such as a *thermionic valve*, television tube or *transistor*.

Energy The ability of something to produce activity. Petrol or diesel fuel produce energy when the car starts, electricity produces energy when a light is turned on.

Floppy disc Small, removable magnetic disc, made of coated plastic and usually in a plastic case, used to store computer information and transfer it between computers. The text for this book was stored on a floppy disc.

Fluorescent light Type of electric light in which light is produced by a glowing tube, usually filled with mercury vapour, instead of a white-hot filament, as in a light bulb.

FM (Frequency Modulation) Way of transmitting sound using radio signals, by varying the *frequency* of the *radio wave* to match the electrical signal from the microphone.

Frequency The number of times per second any repetitive change occurs, such as the rate at which a lighthouse flashes or a *radio wave* changes.

Fuse Electrical safety device consisting of a thin piece of wire in a glass tube. The wire overheats and melts if too much *electricity* flows through it. This breaks the electrical circuit, so preventing damage to electrical equipment.

Hard disc Magnetic disc, usually made of coated metal, which is fixed inside a computer and used to store information such as computer programs.

Hertz Measure of frequency; one hertz equals one change per second. Named after the German physicist, Heinrich Hertz.

Hologram Special type of photograph, taken with *laser* light, in which objects appear to have real depth, unlike ordinary photographs.

Infra-red rays Form of *electromagnetic radiation* that is invisible, but can be felt as heat.

Insulator Material through which *electricity* cannot pass, such as plastic, wood and ceramics.

Integrated circuit Piece of *semiconductor* material, usually silicon, on which a large number of electronic circuits have been etched.

Intelsat The International Telecommunications Satellite Organization, which set up and maintains a global communications satellite network.

Laser A device which produces a powerful, focussed beam of light, which can be used to cut or weld materials, or to transmit *telecommunications* signals.

LCD (Liquid Crystal Display) A thin sandwich of plastic and Liquid Crystal, a substance which darkens when an electric current passes through it. LCDs are used to display letters and numbers in devices such as watches, calculators and portable computers.

LED (Light Emitting Diode) A *semiconductor* which glows when an electric current passes through it.

Long Wave Waveband of radio signals, used for *AM* radio broadcasts and navigational ship-to-shore communication. Long-wave radio stations have a worldwide range.

Magnetic field The distribution of a magnetic force through space.

Maxwell's Laws These describe how *electromagnetic radiation* travels through space. They were discovered by the Scottish physicist James Clerk Maxwell in the 1860s.

Medium Wave Waveband of radio signals used for *AM* radio broadcasts and communication between ships. Medium-wave radio stations have a range of several hundred kilometres.

Microprocessor *Integrated circuit* or 'silicon chip' which contains the Central Processing Unit (CPU) of a computer.

Microwave Waveband of radio signals used for telecommunication satellites, radar and microwave ovens.

Modulation Adding electrical information signals (such as signals from a microphone) to a *carrier wave*, to transmit information or *video signals*.

Mouse Hand-operated device which allows the user to move a cursor around the screen of a computer, to select information on programs or to draw lines.

Negative In a photographic negative light and dark are reversed, so when the negative is printed, by placing it over photographic paper and exposing it to light, a 'normal' picture is produced.

Optical fibres Long, thin glass cables which can transmit light over long distances. They are used to carry *telecommunications* signals.

Pentaprism Piece of glass with five faces used in single-lens reflex cameras to turn the image in the viewfinder upright and the right way round.

Photo-electric cell See *Solar cell*.

Photoresistant layer Thin layer of material used in making *integrated circuits*, which hardens when exposed to *ultraviolet light*.

Radio waves Form of *electromagnetic radiation* used in *telecommunications*.

Receiver Device used to convert electric signals into sound and pictures, such as a television receiver, radio receiver, radar receiver or telephone receiver.

Semiconductor Material, such as silicon, germanium or gallium arsenide, which does not conduct electricity unless 'doped' with another material. See also *diode* and *transistor*.

Short wave Waveband of radio signals used for *AM* radio broadcasts, amateur radio and communications with ships and aircraft.

Silicon chip See *Integrated circuit*.

Smart card Card similar to a bank card which incorporates an integrated circuit containing detailed information about the user, such as signature, photograph, personal details and/or financial transactions.

Solar cell Device to convert light into *electricity*. Large solar cells power satellites, small ones work pocket calculators.

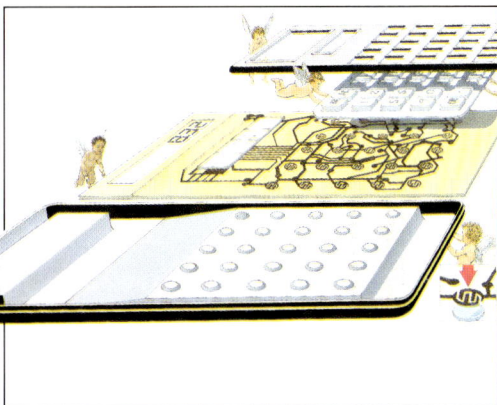

Sound wave The pattern of pressure changes in air, water or other materials which we hear as sound.

Spectrum The complete range of wavelengths of *electromagnetic radiation*.

Synchronizing signal Tiny signal that ensures that two distant pieces of equipment, such as a television transmitter and receiver, are operating together.

Telecommunication Communication over a distance by radio signals or through wires, cables and *optical fibre* cables.

Telegraph System for transmitting messages through wires and cables by on-off electrical signals.

Teleprinter Machine for transmitting telegraph messages as they are typed (keyed in) and printing out the messages received.

Thermionic valve Early electronic device used for switching and amplifying electrical signals. Now replaced by *semiconductors*.

Transformer Device that increases or decreases the voltage of *AC electricity*.

Transistor Small electronic device made of *semiconductor* material which amplifies electric signals and also switches them on and off.

Transmitter (radio) Device connected to an aerial which broadcasts *radio waves*.

Tuning Adjusting a radio *receiver* or a television set to select signals from a particular *transmitter*.

Turbine Type of engine in which jets of steam, burning gas or water flow over blades attached to a shaft, turning it to drive electric generators, propellers or other machinery.

UHF Ultra-high frequency radio waves, used to transmit television signals and radio signals.

Ultraviolet light *Electromagnetic radiation*, invisible to the naked eye, with a *wavelength* shorter than visible light.

VHF Very high frequency radio waves used for *FM* radio broadcasts and short-range communication (eg the police).

Video System for recording and replaying *video signals*.

Video signals Electric signals containing moving picture information.

Vidicon tube Electronic device that scans a picture, converting it into an electrical signal.

Volt Measure of electrical *energy*; named after the Italian scientist Alessandro Volta.

Waveband Range of radio waves of similar wavelength or frequency.

Wavelength The distance between two successive wave crests, or similar points, in a row of waves.

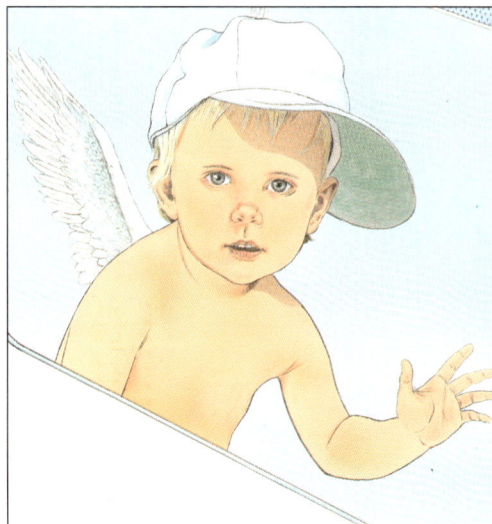

INDEX

proost
PRINTED IN BELGIUM BY
INTERNATIONAL BOOK PRODUCTION